WITNESS TO THE WORLD BEYOND

WITNESS TO THE WORLD BEYOND

KEVIN V. COAN

AN EVIDENTIAL MEDIUM

Barbara Ellen Mawn

Witness to the World Beyond is a work of nonfiction, an authorized biography of Kevin V. Coan. Actual real names are used in certain cases with permission only. Some of the names and geographic locations have been changed to protect the privacy of people whose stories are included in this book.

Copyright © 2024 by Barbara Ellen Mawn

www.barbaraellenmawn.com

Book cover design: Nathan Hayward
www.vividedge.org

Author photo: Cynthia August
www.cynthiaaugust.com

Makeup artist for author photo: Lynne Avallone

No part of this book may be reproduced, shared, distributed, downloaded or stored via any type of system (recording, electronic, mechanical, photocopying or other means) without the prior permission of the author. Your support of the author's rights is appreciated.

All Rights Reserved
Printed in the United States of America
First Edition

ISBN 979-8-9901346-0-7

FOR NELLIE PARSONS MAWN

My Irish paternal grandmother whose life
has inspired this work
and my creative impulse to write

AND

FOR CATHERINE O'BRIEN
MCAVOY

My maternal grandmother who passed
away when my own mother was only three
years old, but whose presence I felt
strongly during my mother's last day on
this earth

Table of Contents

FOREWORD XI

PART I: THE BOY WHO LOVED TO FLY XV

CHAPTER 1: THE EARLY YEARS.. 1
CHAPTER 2: FINDING HIS WAY ON PLANES AND TRAINS 11

PART II: THE SPOOKS COME KNOCKING 15

CHAPTER 3: THE AWAKENING 17
CHAPTER 4: LEARNING THE ROPES ....,,,,.. 21
CHAPTER 5: JEALOUSY AND COMPETITION IN THE FIELD.................... 28
CHAPTER 6: GETTING BACK IN FLIGHT... 33
CHAPTER 7: HOW DOES THE PROCESS WORK?................................. 36
CHAPTER 8: LIVING LIFE ON HIS OWN TERMS 79

PART III: EVIDENCE FROM THE "REAL MCCOY" 87

CHAPTER 9: "FROZEN IN GRIEF," LEARNING TO LIVE AGAIN AFTER THE
LOSS OF A CHILD 89
CHAPTER 10: THE CONTINUITY OF LIFE – A BIT OF COMFORT AND PEACE
.... 110
CHAPTER 11: FORGIVENESS, IT'S NOT YOUR FAULT......................... 128
CHAPTER 12: THE ILLUSORY NATURE OF TIME................................ 139
CHAPTER 13: THE CYNICS AND THE SKEPTICS 158
CHAPTER 14: "YOU CAN'T MAKE THIS STUFF UP"- MORE VALIDATION
STORIES 187

PART IV: THE IMPACT OF RELIGION AND PERSONAL VISITS
FROM SPIRITS... 215

CHAPTER 15: RELIGIOUS INFLUENCES ON MEDIUMSHIP BELIEFS 217
CHAPTER 16: MESSAGES FROM BEYOND, NOT AS UNCOMMON AS YOU
MIGHT THINK 223

AFTERWORD 247

ACKNOWLEDGEMENTS... 253

Foreword

This book is an authorized biography of medium Kevin V. Coan. After I had a reading with Kevin in the fall of 2020, I casually commented, "Your ability is amazing; you really should write a book." That was not the first time he had heard this suggestion, but he had neither the time nor interest to write a book. I spontaneously offered to write it myself and our partnership began.

Unlike some modern-day mediums, Kevin is not an attention seeker. He has done his best to avoid fame and fortune associated with his ability as a medium. He agreed to the book hesitantly at first as he enjoys his privacy and quiet life with friends and family. His purpose in collaborating with this book was to share his stories and help people to understand what mediumship is about. It is a validation of his ability to communicate with people who have died, an ability that he was vaguely aware of since his early childhood. He has no interest in converting any non-believers of mediumship. He is secure in the knowledge that he has people who trust in his abilities across the globe. Kevin has been told countless times that he has made an enormous difference in people's lives. For over twenty-five years, Kevin V. Coan has provided a sense of peace and closure for those who have lost loved ones.

The materials in the book are based on in-depth individual interviews with Kevin, twenty-three people who have had readings by him and two who are personally connected to him but have not been read by him. In addition, I observed ninety-seven readings that Kevin conducted in six open public sessions. All names are aliases in this book unless permission was granted to use the real name. You may wonder how a former academic and nurse researcher happened to take on this project. Well, that explanation goes a way back…

My grandmother, Ellen (Nellie) Parsons Mawn emigrated from County Roscommon, Ireland, arriving in Boston on May 20, 1907. She was seventeen years old and traveled alone on the ship SS Cymric. Her plan was to live with her older sister who was already settled and living in Winchester, MA, a suburb of Boston. According to her ship's manifest, Nellie arrived carrying a net worth of four US dollars; she intended to support herself by working as a housekeeper in America.

Several years later, Nellie sought out the services of a local tea-leaf reader. She wanted to know if she would get married. Her tea-leaf fortune teller told her not to worry, she would marry a man in uniform that she would first lay eyes on when she looked over her own left shoulder at a dance.

My grandmother would later marry Thomas (Tom) Mawn in 1912. He too had emigrated from Ireland, leaving his home in county Leitrim by himself in 1908 on the SS Saxonia with seven dollars and fifty cents to his name. He had a brother who was waiting for him in Dorchester, MA. Nellie and Tom met at a local dance for Irish immigrants one evening outside of Boston and reportedly Tom was indeed first seen by Nellie when she looked over her left shoulder. Tom was wearing his horse drawn trolley car uniform. Power of persuasion? Perhaps. Power of imagination? Perhaps. Power of the ability to see future events by the tea reader? Perhaps.

Nellie Mawn was also reputed to be an expert tea leaf reader herself later on but gave it up at some point mid-life when she saw a disturbing death of the husband of a woman that she was reading. The woman could see that Nellie was visibly upset as she examined the patterns of her tea leaves; the woman demanded to know what Nellie saw. Nellie did not tell her but the woman suspected tragedy ahead from Nellie's facial expressions. The woman's husband was later killed in an accident and she never spoke to Nellie again.

Nellie had completed the fifth grade and Tom's highest level of education was the fourth grade. They both were literate and bilingual (Gaelic and English) however. Despite his lack of formal schooling, my grandfather started his own small, but successful oil delivery business in the U.S. after he saved enough money from various jobs driving trolleys and trucks. They had four children, the youngest being my father, Everett, who attained a high school education and enjoyed a successful business career. He and my mother had seven children and the third generation of U.S. Mawns were all college educated with several attaining advanced degrees.

As a young girl, I would smirk at our immigrant grandmother's claims of being able to see a world which was not visible. Not only did we hear about her tea leaf reading abilities, she loved to tease us about fairies and leprechauns. It was hard to know what was real and what wasn't at times in their household. Since then, throughout my career as a nurse, I have tended to people of all ages during their final hours in many different settings during the past four decades. I have observed many unexplainable phenomena as people endured the dying process.

xiii

In my early forties, I also experienced various forms of messages and signs from beyond starting after my own mother passed in 1995. Thus, my working experiences as a nurse for over thirty years and the experience of the loss of many dear family members are consistent with my belief in our ancestors' desire and ability to commune with us, despite a doctoral degree in social policy with a focus on research data. I have no need or inclination to convince any reader of this; I simply wanted to share the stories and shed light on one man's remarkable life journey as a medium.

Part I: The Boy Who Loved to Fly

*"All happy families are alike;
each unhappy family is unhappy in its own
way."*

Leo Tolstoy (1877)

*"I can't say I've had a miserable childhood
but it certainly wasn't the easiest or the best."*

Kevin Coan (2020)

Chapter 1: The Early Years

Kevin V. Coan's parents never once held a birthday party for him during his childhood. Given any complaint or injury, his mother's response was, "You'll live." When he was in the second grade, he fell off a swing set and went to his mother complaining of excruciating arm pain. She ignored it until ten days later when his arm had started to set on its own in an obviously deformed way. She finally brought him to see a doctor and they were told it would now require surgery, a re-breaking of the bone and then resetting of the arm. Yes, "he lived," but this is one example of many that revealed her lack of tenderness and sense of motherly protection for her son as a young child. As he recalled this story, he laughed softly and said, "Well, that's not really exactly attentive parenting."

"Why can't you be a normal boy and put a ball in your hand instead of a book?" his mother sighed in frustration one day. His father overheard her and got so frustrated himself seeing his seven-year-old son sitting in the house on a weekend reading a book that he left the room to get a putty knife. He then proceeded to tear the book to shreds with the knife.

As a young child, Kevin's parents did not realize that he had any unusual abilities beyond being a very good clarinet player and budding photographer. There were a few signs in hindsight, his mother later realized, but they attributed his strange ways at times to having "invisible" friends as a young boy. In other instances, they simply ignored and did not acknowledge some of his other unexplainable behaviors.

The Spirits started coming to Kevin through his bedroom wall at night, when he was about four years old. It wasn't often, maybe four or five times during his childhood that he recalled.

"Oh yes, it was absolutely frightening, I remember it being very loud. It was not like they are trying to harm you or anything like that, but I remember it being very loud."

But for the most part of his young life, he didn't really think about these noisy visitors. It did not define his childhood in any way as he became accustomed to it on rare occasions. When he would hear the loud talking, he would sometimes run to his parents in the kitchen or their bedroom. He would often be talking with these invisible forces.

"I couldn't understand why they weren't understanding what I was talking about. I just remember getting so frustrated because they would just be laughing at me and laughing at me…but I went off somewhere."

At the time his parents thought he was crazy, that he had experienced a bad dream, or that he had an invisible friend. They did not understand it and had no reason to think it was anything beyond a normal childhood nightmare.

Kevin V. Coan was the second child in a family with four children and the only son of Janice and Charles Coan. He was born in Beverly, Massachusetts (MA), a small coastal town on the North Shore, an area in northeastern Massachusetts. He lived in Danvers, MA, a suburb north of Boston, in his earliest years. The family then moved to Hamilton, MA, a suburban, somewhat rural town twenty-seven miles north of Boston during the majority of his primary school years and for the remainder of his childhood. Kevin was a major source of disappointment to his parents as a young boy.

Kevin describes himself as "one hundred percent Irish." His paternal great grandfather emigrated from Ireland in 1878 and married a woman who also hailed from the old sod. On his mother's side, his great, great grandparents had emigrated from Ireland. Both of his parents were raised initially in Peabody, MA, a working-class city north of Boston. Later his father's family moved to Melrose, MA.

Kevin's parents met at a country club dance in Salem, MA, when Charles was twenty-four and Janice was twenty-two. They married on October 12, 1957. Both parents were college graduates. Janice majored in elementary education at Leslie College (now University) and taught in an elementary school early on; later in life she worked as a medical secretary for an oncology ward and in radiation services at a local hospital. Charles Coan was a graduate of Boston College and worked as an oil company salesman for many years.

As a young child, Kevin recalled his father often being under the influence of alcohol. It was not a pleasant memory. Charles Coan lost his job due to his drinking problem when Kevin was in junior high school.

Eventually the disease would kill him at age fifty-six. By the time Kevin reached the sixth grade, he was aware that his mother was also an alcoholic. His parents loved to entertain and often had large parties; Kevin would disappear into his room and read to escape the loud noise.

"There would be like fifty people downstairs and I'd just stay up in my room. I was very happy being left alone and up in my room. And so, I've been that way ever since."

Kevin could only recall spending two occasions together as a child with just his father – attending a St. Patrick's Day parade in Boston one year and going to a Red Sox baseball game a few years later. Both days were a bit of a bore to Kevin. There was nothing he could do to please his father. Being a disappointment was one thing to deal with, being raised by two alcoholic parents was a more monumental hurdle for a child.

Kevin was not a particularly popular kid in school but he typically had two to three good friends. He acknowledges that he has pretty much been an introvert since his early childhood. He was smart, quiet, loved to read and was interested in photography and airplanes as a young boy. Kevin had no interest in sports and played clarinet in the band much to his father's embarrassment. He rarely got in trouble. He was not your typical "all American boy."

Since he was five years old, Kevin Coan has been fascinated with airplanes. He knew early on that when he grew up, he wanted to work around planes. The father of Bob, one of Kevin's childhood best friends, was a ramp agent for American Airlines, responsible for the handling of luggage, cargo and mail. He encouraged Kevin's interest and since his own father had little use for him, Kevin hero-worshipped this man. During one sleepover

Technology (MIT) which was a rather unusual accomplishment for those of Irish descent back then.

Kevin's sister Kathy acknowledged that there was dysfunction in the family.

"Growing up, we thought that was the norm. You have more perspective when you get older, you realize that things might not have been ... normal."

Kevin's father took on a coaching role in the Little League with the hope of encouraging his son to play. His mother colluded with her husband and forced Kevin to "join" the team and dress in uniform for the games even though he hadn't gone through the tryout process. He played so poorly that his father wouldn't even use him. This was all his mother's doing and why she did it was beyond Kevin's imagination. He came home from school one day and was told he could no longer be on the team, with no reasons given. That was fine by him but his mother still insisted that he attend the game in uniform that evening nonetheless.

"It's fine you don't want me on the team but don't make me go!" he pleaded. He lost that argument; it was one of the more embarrassing moments of his childhood.

Kevin was initially raised as a Catholic, although his parents stopped attending church regularly in his early childhood. He became an altar boy nonetheless as he found attending Mass boring but at least if you had something to do, it was bearable. It got him out of the house. And the perks included an annual trip such as a day at Canobie Lake Park, a small amusement park in New Hampshire. He was soon disillusioned by the Church and in particular, by the local priest who was also "a mean drunk." He was not aware of any sexual abuse happening in the Church as a child. Once he made his confirmation

Witness to the World Beyond 5

at Bob's house, the father, Mr. C. said, "Come on, we are going to the airport." This was during the mid-1970s when security was quite lax. The boys got to sit in the cockpit of a 747 that had just landed in Boston from Chicago. They were introduced to several pilots and the crew. Kevin was in his glory. He was in the sixth grade by then and all he knew was that there was a man on this earth paying attention to him and it certainly was not his father. He also realized that he wanted to work on a plane when he grew up.

With the chaos created by his parents' drinking, only once in his life, while in the eighth grade, did he dare to ask a friend to a sleepover at his house. Bob was invited to come over but had to be sent home when news of Kevin's grandfather's death came that day. It was his father's father, Charles Sr., whom Kevin recalled as a nice man. He never invited anyone to a sleepover again.

"I remember the one time I was going to have someone over, somebody died," he commented with a small grin.

Kevin's paternal grandmother lived well into her eighties. After her husband died, she continued to live in the same house with her sister, Kevin's great Aunt Irene, who never married, and her son Gerry, Kevin's uncle, about twenty miles away from Kevin's family home. On occasion, Kevin would stay with them when things got tough at home but as he recalled, that grandmother was "not the warmest person." His maternal grandmother, Margaret, died when Kevin was only five years old but he recalled she was very nice to him. His maternal grandfather passed away before his parents even married so he was never a part of Kevin's life. That grandfather had a reputation of being a brilliant but rather mean man. He was a graduate of the Massachusetts Institute of

Witness to the World Beyond   7

in the eighth grade, he announced that he was done with the Catholic Church.

His mother insisted, "Well, you're going to church."

Kevin responded, "Well, you get dressed, we can all go as a family. You're coming with us. You are going to set an example."

His mother then "shut up" about it and he never attended Sunday Mass in the Catholic Church again.

One of the unexplainable incidents during his childhood happened sometime around the fourth or fifth grade. Kevin was sitting in the school auditorium waiting for the school bus to arrive along with several hundred other students.

As he explained, "All of a sudden, I looked around and there's nobody there. Next thing I know I'm sitting alone in the auditorium and the principal's secretary came up and said, 'We lost you for a while.' I guess I didn't respond. They tried to wake me up but my eyes were open. I just went somewhere else. I just don't know where."

The principal called his mother to pick him up, explaining the strange occurrence. His mother normally would have been furious if he missed the bus for any reason, causing her to have to pick him up. He recalled that she wasn't mad this time.

"My mother didn't say anything. She just picked me up in the car, we drove home and it was never discussed again."

His mother never talked about the incident with any doctor, teacher or school administrator from that day forward.

As Kevin got older, things continued to get worse at home.

"My father really disliked me. I couldn't even stay at home. I was working three jobs. Nothing I would do could please my father. It was bad. I never took a drug in my life. I never took a drink in my life. I didn't get into any trouble. Most parents would be thrilled to have a kid that worked three jobs. No, not my parents."

But Kevin made the best of it and found friendship and support outside of the home with his small group of close friends, a few of their parents and his co-workers. His friend Bob would go on to a different high school but one of the other "unpopular" kids, David, who was "a brain," would become his best friend in his freshman year of high school.

"I practically lived at David's house. David's mother was like a second mother to me." Kevin spent very little time at his own house and very rarely invited friends over to his house for any reason because of the potential chaos that might ensue with his parents' drinking problem.

One of his first jobs in high school was at a local supermarket. He and another friend, Alex, worked together at the grocery store where they developed a group of friends that they would socialize with after the store closed on weekends. At age sixteen, Kevin worked thirty-nine hours per week – essentially full time but without benefits since it was under forty hours. He had signed up for a work study program that allowed him to work at the supermarket from twelve noon to nine in the evening while still attending high school.

Kevin's relationship with his parents was never an easy road. Times were often tough economically but they managed to hold on to their modest home. After his father was fired from his job in the oil industry, his mother had

Witness to the World Beyond   9

to go back to work in various secretarial positions at local hospitals. While they didn't go on family vacations even when his father was employed, his parents did occasionally manage to travel together to faraway places such as London and Spain. They would "pawn" the four kids on rather dubious babysitters for the week. "They weren't the best...." caretakers, Kevin recalled with a wry smile.

The one thing about Kevin that his mother was proud of during his childhood was his membership in the high school band. He played clarinet in one of the best marching bands in the state at the time. They played at the football games and his mother would watch him play in the band, but never once did his father come.

"He was probably embarrassed that I was in the band instead of being on the football field, even though the team was terrible."

Later in his adult life, his mother would also become proud of his mediumship ability as he came into his own but this was not recognized or understood during his childhood.

As Kevin got to the end of his high school years, his parents never asked him if he was interested in going to college. They never encouraged him or discussed what he wanted to do with his life. He decided on his own to apply to a local community college. He would not last long there as he realized that he needed to live independently, away from his parents, which would require working full time. His mother was angry with him for quitting college and leaving home. At the age of eighteen, they had started to charge him fifty dollars per week for rent which was "a lot of money in those days." Beyond the rent, his relationship with his parents, particularly his father, made it untenable to live at home any longer. It was time to move on.

On his deathbed, his father confided to one of his friends, "My biggest regret in life is how I treated my son. If I had to do it over again, I would've been so much better to him."

This remorse he shared with a co-worker who later shared it with family members. But it was too little, too late, for Kevin. He felt nothing at the news of his father's death.

Chapter 2: Finding His Way on Planes and Trains

Kevin's passion for the airline industry has never waned since childhood. Being a medium was not on his radar in his early twenties as he was unaware of what his abilities were. His "number one goal" as a young adult was to find a way to work for the airlines.

"It was so in my blood; I can't even tell you. To this day, the whole industry fascinates me like nothing else."

After completing high school and soon thereafter quitting college, Kevin went to work in a local bank as a teller. This was in the late 1970s and it was very difficult to get any job in the airline industry. He used to drive to Boston from his apartment in the North Shore area of Massachusetts to take pictures of planes from the various airlines. As luck would have it, his bank position led him to an opportunity that was created by his own ingenuity. Air New England at the time was a small local airline. He found out that the chief executive officer (CEO) of Air New England lived in his town, and that the CEO's wife was a regular customer at his bank. He asked the other three tellers to close their windows when she came in at the same time and day each week, so that she'd be forced to go to his window. He "charmed the hell out of her" over the course of several weeks. Finally, he mentioned that he noticed her husband worked for Air New England and he wondered if she could ask her husband about his job application that he hadn't heard back from.

"I'll ask him when he comes home tonight. How did you know my husband works for Air New England?" the wife of the CEO asked.

Very quickly he responded, "Oh, it looked like you deposited a pay check and so… I just assumed."

She came in the very next day and said, "No banking business today but I wanted to let you know, you have an interview."

Kevin worked there for three years, eventually getting laid off as the business began to falter and was forced to return to a bank and/or other jobs outside the airline industry. After his Air New England experience, at one point he worked briefly at a New York airline, but didn't stay long as they had poor working conditions.

Next, Kevin worked in a series of jobs for several years, often two to three jobs at a time including working in a vault in a Boston bank, a travel agency, and Sears. He also became a telephone operator for two years during this time period and achieved the distinction of being the "fastest operator in the United States." He was having trouble finding a job back in the airlines so his second choice was working on a train. But his application was going nowhere at Amtrak; it was "another company that just never hired."

And then a bit of serendipity helped him once again. His old landlord from Marblehead, MA, would occasionally forward his mail a few times per month to his new address in Lynn, MA. One day when he came home in June of 1983, he found a forwarded letter dated April of that year that had invited him to an interview at Amtrak. He immediately called the head of personnel and explained his delayed response, but it was two months too late.

He was told, "I'm so sorry, but we have done all our hiring. We won't be hiring for a couple of years." Kevin was devastated.

Several months later, he was sitting in the bank vault and just had this feeling to call Amtrak back.

"I don't know if you remember me, but I was the applicant whose landlord didn't forward the interview invitation letter to me. I was just checking in."

The head of personnel replied, "I can't believe you're calling me. We're interviewing right now."

His first out of five interviews was then scheduled for the next work day. During the final interview, the regional director got a phone call and apologized that he had to stop the interview at that moment to deal with an emergency. It was a major collision of two trains on Hell Gate Bridge in New York.

When Kevin returned for the follow up interview, the director said, "Well you must really want the job. You came back after a train wreck!"

He got the job and stayed there for nearly seventeen years, working his way up to being a Union Vice President in the organization. It wasn't flying, but it was the next best thing to working in the airline industry.

Part II: The Spooks Come Knocking

"During my own quest for truth, I have run the gamut of emotions from amusement to semi-belief; from disillusionment, to an awakening awareness that the human mind and the so-called hereafter are the greatest unexplored reaches for the adventurous man."

Ruth Montgomery (1967)

Chapter 3: The Awakening

Within three years after starting the Amtrak job, Kevin, now age twenty-six, decided to celebrate his birthday by going out to dinner with his friend John. John had shared with Kevin that he was a psychic and invited Kevin to come to his church, the oldest Spiritualist Church in America in Salem, MA, after the birthday dinner.

In 1926, Sir Arthur Conan Doyle, famous for his Sherlock Holmes series, wrote a two-volume book entitled "The History of Spiritualism." He described the Spiritualist Movement as "...the most important [movement] in the world since the Christ episode." While he acknowledged that spiritualists, or those who believe in "preternatural interference" (communication from the dead), have existed since time immemorial, he noted that the "modern" Spiritualist movement could be traced to the writings of Emanuel Swedenborg, a Swedish seer, writer and philosopher from the mid 1700s. Sir Conan Doyle referred to him as "the first and greatest of modern mediums."

The Spiritualist Church itself was founded a century later in 1848 but immediately sought to distance itself from Swedenborg's work according to Doyle. The new prophetic medium who is generally given credit for this movement was an unassuming, uneducated and poor man, Andrew Jackson Davis from New York state. Mr. Davis reported that he had heard a voice telling him that he would act as a prophet for "the good work that has begun" on March 31, 1848 which is generally recognized as the birth of the modern Spiritualist Church. There are now thousands of Spiritualist Churches across the world, predominantly in English speaking countries. There are at least fourteen Spiritualist Churches listed in Massachusetts alone.

Kevin had occasionally gone to psychics himself to see if he could figure out when and how he would ever return to flying again, even though he was satisfied with the Amtrak position for many years. Kevin's mother and aunt were also interested in visiting psychics when he was growing up and his mother once mentioned that he had a great aunt who had psychic abilities as well. It was not a far-fetched idea in his mind although he was skeptical of most psychics and mediums whom he considered charlatans. Nonetheless, he agreed to check out the Spiritualist Church with his friend that evening with the hope that he might get a reading on his future job prospects in the airline industry. He didn't get a reading that night but was intrigued with the Church's beliefs in the paranormal.

At a subsequent visit to the Spiritualist Church, the main speaker one evening was the Church Pastor, a medium in her eighties named Gladys Worsencroft. She pointed to Kevin during the service and said, "Dear, Spirit wants to work with you and they want you to get into unfoldment classes." In these classes sponsored by the Church, they trained people to develop their medium abilities. At the time he had no desire or interest. But he remained captivated by what he observed that evening and started attending more frequently.

One day soon after, he was hanging out with his friend again when John realized that he had to leave soon to go to his unfoldment class. "You should come to class with me."

"I don't want to go to class with you. You know what? You go and I'll take a walk along the ocean on Lynn Shore Drive."

Kevin was not interested in becoming a medium at that point. He did not think of his occasional childhood visions as being anything out of the ordinary or something to explore.

Months later, while working for Amtrak, he had an overnight trip to Washington DC. It was near dawn and he hadn't slept well that night in the hotel. He had to leave in a few hours but still couldn't get to sleep. He was lying awake on the bed, wishing he could get in just a short nap before he had to get up and go back to work. He recalled that he felt funny, strangely odd, not sick, but it was an unexplainable, weird sensation. He looked down at the foot of the bed and there were three Spirits standing there.

"I remember staring at them for about thirty seconds. And then I remember looking up at the ceiling and saying, 'Oh please, not tonight.' And I looked down and they were gone."

He didn't tell a soul about this vision. That evening after he got home, he decided to attend the Spiritualist Church service. Once again, the medium Pastor Gladys W. was there.

This time she pointed to Kevin and said, "Dear, I need to speak to you. Spirits came to visit you last night and you asked them to leave. They want to get you into class and are getting very impatient with you."

After the service ended it was customary to thank the speaker with a hug and a peck on the cheek. When it was Kevin's turn to do so, she once again warned, "You get into class or they'll be back."

That was the catalyst for Kevin to become a medium. He had seen the Spirits as a child on rare occasions but it was not something that he paid much attention to. But he knew he did not want to "piss them off."

"Not everybody is called to it," he concluded. "A lot of people (mediums and psychics) just want to cash in but they don't have the goods to back it up." At this point, he realized that he may have the goods and that he could be of use to others.

Chapter 4: Learning the Ropes

Soon after Kevin's realization that he had this ability, he met another medium, Mary Maguire, at a Spiritualist Church service. She was a Spiritualist minister who was licensed to teach an unfoldment class but at this Church, she was not allowed to do so. It had to do with jealousy, as she was an incredible medium with much stronger powers to communicate with the dead than the other mediums affiliated with the church at the time.

She came up to Kevin at a church service and said, "I'm having a class at my house and I'm not asking you, I'm telling you that you're going to be in my class."

He decided to show up and subsequently learned how to develop his abilities very quickly over the next few years under Mary's tutelage.

"It was just absolutely wonderful…I liked the people in the class…no egos."

Although Kevin learned to develop his ability relatively easily, at first, he had doubts. "I would sit there and say I don't know why I'm coming. I'm not getting anything anyway. I don't meditate and the first thing everybody does in class is meditate for like thirty minutes. That was a killer for me because it felt like hours."

And then he recalled his first reading. "I remember it was all of a sudden, I remember picking up Spirit. I turned to Mary and told her that she had thrown a dead plant in the wastebasket in the bedroom upstairs that day and her father was with her."

She replied, "I did, that's exactly what I did."

That was a pivotal point for Kevin, "That's when I knew I was on to something. And so, every week it started to get stronger and stronger. And they [the Spirits] just started working with me effortlessly, thank God, because if I had to put any work into this, I wouldn't do it."

Kevin's sister Kathy recalled Kevin's apprenticeship with Mary, "I know that she was a very important person to Kevin. He really wanted to study with Mary to find out what this…I don't think Kevin would call it a gift, what this ability meant and its responsibility. I think he truly understands how important this is to people and I don't think he takes it lightly."

Although he is not one for advance meditation to prepare himself for readings, it does take an enormous strain on him physically and mentally.

"It is very, very, very exhausting…if I do ten readings, I make it home and within fifteen minutes I'm dead asleep."

One of Kevin's first readings in the North Shore area was at a house in Gloucester, MA. A friend had referred him to this couple who had just completed building their new home.

The first thing that Kevin told them was, "There is something wrong with your oil burner."

"That's impossible," replied the husband, "this is a brand-new house! It's only a few months old!"

"Well, there is something wrong with it," Kevin replied.

The husband again scoffed and replied, "You couldn't be more wrong."

Three weeks later their oil burner burst; there was soot everywhere. No one was injured luckily. The wife later told her friends with a laugh, "Thanks to Kevin, he's ruined my marriage. We go out and that's all my husband wants to do – talk about Kevin!"

This scenario often happens and he is known for not backing down with the information he gets from Spirit. If someone doesn't understand or disagrees with a comment from a reading, he simply says, "Take it with you, remember I mentioned it."

He acknowledged that he tells that to people all the time and then more often than not... "Bang – it later happens! It gets crazy."

While he does not consider himself a psychic who can see into the future, he noted that sometimes he is given a message from Spirit and he cannot be sure of its relation to time. One time he recalled that while he was sitting at a book store drinking a cup of coffee, he had just opened his book to read and relax when he thought, "Oh shit! My water heater just blew!"

He left for home immediately where the water was flowing everywhere from his attic water heater. He was rather annoyed Spirit didn't give more advance warning on that but on the other hand, he acknowledged that the flooding would have been much, much worse if he had gone home hours later as planned. More to follow on the illusive nature of timing in some of his readings in Chapter 12.

In the early years of his development as a medium, Kevin was somewhat horrified to realize that he could get

24 Barbara Ellen Mawn

information at times from Spirit that was unwelcomed. For example, he went to a local small amusement park in New Hampshire one day. While he was standing in line for one of the rides, he "picked up" that the young woman in front of him would die in a car accident. She'd be with a man in the car who would survive the crash. He wasn't sure how or when or where. He didn't think that this would happen; he knew it would happen. He tried to put it out of his thoughts and focus on something else.

Later that same day, he found himself again behind her in a line for an amusement ride and the vision vividly returned to him. He realized that he could not alarm her with this information. Even if she didn't think him insane for telling her this, he had no way to help her to avoid her fate.

He begged Spirit later that night, "Please don't ever do that again. I don't want to hear it," unless, he clarified, he was in the act of doing a reading and there was some possible way that he might be able to prevent such a tragedy.

For the most part, Spirit has since allowed him to be free of unwanted interference from people's lives who are simply walking down the street near him. He has learned to control his ability and his relationship with Spirit so that his own life is not a constant source of terror and information overload.

As he began to meet others with similar abilities and those interested in such phenomena, he was invited to a "table tipping" by a friend named Phyllis from the Spiritualist Church. Table tipping involves a medium harnessing energy from a spirit that results in the movement of a table (or other object), without forcibly moving it by hand, technology or trickery. According to the Netflix docuseries, "Surviving Death," based on the book by Leslie Keen, the Society for Psychical Research at Cambridge University in Oxford, England, recognizes this type of mediumship as a physical vs. mental type of mediumship, with the latter type referring to communication with the dead via various senses through the mind. Physical mediumship was more commonly documented early in the Spiritualist Movement in the 1800s during seances and other spiritualist activities but can still be found in some Spiritualist centers today.

Kevin was aware of the meaning of table tipping but was still learning about harnessing the energy from Spirit in the more common way, through his senses, and at first had no desire to participate. After three calls asking him to come, he finally relented, figuring he would observe what it was all about. It turned out that he was the only medium that showed up for the evening.

> "So, we got to the salon where the table tipping was to commence. The table was like the size of an end table. We sat around it, all scrunched together. Everyone put two fingers from each hand on top of the table. The idea is that eventually the vibration will be picked up and Spirit will move the table. So anyway, we sat there. I just remember the table was a little bit low and I remember my back was killing me. We sat there probably for an hour and half. But what happened is that all of a sudden, I saw a nun walk in the room and I said her name. Phyllis recognized her name. She exclaimed, 'Oh my God, she was a client of mine! She passed away about a year ago!' And so, the nun was there in spirit as an apparition. And all of a sudden, the table started to shake and rock back and forth. I mean big time! We're talking rocking! For whatever reason, Phyllis got up from the table and

walked to the back of the salon. She just stood against the back wall. Well next thing you know, the table FLEW across the salon! I would say about forty miles per hour. I said, 'Oh my God, it's going to hit Phyllis!' And all of a sudden, the table just stopped and dropped, right in front of Phyllis, about an inch away from her."

Phyllis was unhurt in the commotion. Kevin went on to explain that it was a fun night with an unexpected and exciting ending. But he attributed it to the group being all like-minded people who worked together to get that table to fly. He wasn't impressed with himself, being the only medium there and the one to see the nun spirit…it was truly a group effort. He hasn't tried any forms of physical mediumship since; he prefers to focus on readings with people in individual or groups sessions. The event did enhance his own awareness of the power of the Spirit guides.

Another example of physical movement of property by a Spirit was experienced by one of Kevin's clients. She shared the story with him on her first visit with him. A year prior, her son had died unexpectantly at a young age and she was overcome with grief. A friend of hers gave her Kevin's card and recommended that she set up a reading with him. She put the card in her coat pocket and never followed through or even thought about it again until a year later. At that time, she was still experiencing profound sadness and remembered about the card. She looked in the jacket that she thought she was wearing at the time, but the card was not there. Then she went through all her jackets and pocketbooks, to no avail. That evening she cried and prayed aloud to her deceased son to help her find that card. The next morning, she awoke to find Kevin's business card on her bedside table.

By the early 2000s, Kevin decided to mentor others who were interested in developing medium skills. For approximately three years he held classes with a core group of students at various locations, including a Spiritualist Church, after hours in a hair salon owned by one of the mediumship students and at local community club buildings. Some of the student attendees were known to him from his readings. Several were interested in hearing from lost children by any means possible, even though they did not have the capacity to develop medium abilities themselves. His class ranged in size from ten to thirty students. One attendee in particular progressed well in the enfoldment classes but Kevin was no longer in touch with her to know if she is still using her ability. He stopped teaching enfoldment classes once he returned to full time employment in the airline industry.

Chapter 5: Jealousy and Competition in the Field

Kevin's reputation as a medium started to spread by word of mouth in the North Shore area of Massachusetts during his unfoldment classes with Mary. He soon started doing home readings and was developing a wide network of clients in the community.

"Oh my God I can't believe how accurate you are!" was a frequent compliment to his growing abilities.

At one point, one of the Spiritualists Churches was planning a community Medium Day and one of the church members, Karina, called and invited him to participate. Prior to this, Kevin was not allowed to work on "the platform" at this church since his training had not been held there.

His response was, "Now you want to use me and make money for the church? Absolutely not."

A few weeks later, Kevin went with Karina to a Borders bookstore where a famous medium, who had just published a book, was giving a brief talk followed by a book signing. On the drive to the bookstore, Karina was still trying to get Kevin to help out at the church fundraiser. She acknowledged that there were no good mediums coming and they needed him to get a good draw. She begged him to come so that this event could be one of the biggest fundraisers for her as the event coordinator. He stood his ground and declined the invitation. Karina assumed that they would both attend the author's presentation at the bookstore that day.

As they approached the presentation area in the bookstore, Kevin turned and said, "Come and get me when you're done." He was heading toward the bookstore cafe.

Karina was surprised, "You're not going to stay and listen to this guy?"

"No, he's not going to say anything I don't already know."

During the session break, Karina returned to the cafe where Kevin was enjoying a cup of coffee and reading a book.

"You're amazing, here's a first class medium downstairs and you're up here reading a book!" she exclaimed.

They planned to meet soon after the book reading had ended. As he came down the stairs to find her, he overheard a conversation that she was having with three middle-aged siblings who had recently lost their mother. They were asking her advice on how to find a local medium to help heal their pain after learning about mediumship at the book event. When Kevin came over to her and the family members, Karina did not introduce him to the siblings, and did not recommend him. Instead, she insisted that they come to the upcoming medium day at her Spiritualist Church. Kevin remained silent in front of the siblings but he and Karina argued about it on the ride home.

Kevin started with, "Well now, was that a nice thing to do? You just said you had bad mediums coming to the event."

Karina angrily retorted, "It isn't about them! [the bereaved siblings], it's about making money for the church!"

"That is why you will never be a medium. You know, it's not about you, it's about them and their need."

Kevin was beginning to see that his ability could be a blessing but also a curse at times. That was the end of his relationship with Karina. She would occasionally refer to him as "the perfect mistake."

"Here you have this incredible gift and you don't even care about it. Most people who are into it would kill for that gift!"

Indeed, Karina longed to be a medium herself but just couldn't develop the ability.

Kevin would later realize that there would be a few people who would befriend him for his medium ability primarily. He has always been one who sized up people immediately after meeting them, generally avoiding contact with this type in the future. Some people would also become demanding and expect him to be on call for their life challenges twenty-four/seven. Others would sponsor him for community type shows and then expect that they controlled his mediumship schedule and career. He realized that he would need to make clear boundaries in order to live his life on his own terms. He rarely keeps his phone on and checks it only periodically. He uses a service to make appointments for his readings to minimize unwanted calls.

In addition to the overblown egos that Kevin has witnessed in the medium world, there is the issue of competency and people just making stuff up. Kevin is one of the most vocal critics of those who falsely proclaim to be mediums. And thus, he does not take offense when people are skeptical of him.

> "A lot of mediums take the credit...they are out to make a name for themselves. I can take credit for my time and my standards but I don't have the right to take credit for what I do because if Spirit didn't want to work with me, we might as well sit and sing 'Ninety-nine Bottles of Beer on the Wall' because nothing is going to come through."

Kevin acknowledged that indeed some mediums use tactics that he finds suspect in large crowds. For example, he said they might ask, "Who in here likes cars?" The response might be two hundred people raising their hands. "Anyone can do that." Or similarly, the mediums made famous on TV might be asked, "Do you know the names of your guides?" And of course, Kevin commented that the medium would regurgitate them on the spot, often with rather suspect names like Gabriel.

"Yet all these people lap it right up. I say, can you please find people with the evidence?"

People have often asked Kevin for advice during a reading about what to do as they or family members seem to have some medium abilities. He will recommend going to one of the Spiritualist Churches but with the caveat, "just be careful." He warns people to be cautious because of what he went through.

"I went to hell and back in some of these churches because of my ability."

But at the same time, he met his first teachers and mentors there, Gladys Worsencroft and Mary Maguire, and learned to develop his ability under their mentorship.

So, while he acknowledged that there is the potential for positive outcomes in developing one's ability, he warns people to go into the field with eyes wide open. While he does not compete with other mediums, he noted, "…it tears some people apart if they can't be the best in the room."

Another level of competition among mediums is an online published list of so-called "expert" mediums. On their own initiative, several of Kevin's clients reported to him that they had submitted his name to be added to one of these proprietary sites. Kevin was never contacted from the site developer. Later he learned that it would involve paying fees to get on the list, another source of irritation in this highly competitive world that he chose to ignore.

Chapter 6: Getting Back in Flight

After working almost seventeen years at Amtrak, Kevin was finding himself burned out and exhausted between the demands of the job and part-time medium work. He went on a vacation at this time with a psychic friend to London. They found a Spiritualist meeting house around the corner from another friend's flat. Kevin was the last one to be called on by the medium.

She greeted him with, "Boy, do you hate your job. You know, you actually tell your bosses that they are stupid right to their face."

As a union vice president, he acknowledged, yes, he did that, all the time. She then told him that she saw he would leave his current job in a few months at the beginning of the next year and that the new job would be in transportation. He had indeed been thinking about leaving his job at the end of the year but he wasn't sure if she got it confused that he'd be going into a new transportation job or leaving his current transportation job.

Over the Christmas holiday period, he noticed an advertisement for flight attendants at a small, low budget airline that opened a base of operation in Hanscom Field in Massachusetts in 1999, Shuttle America. He put in a resume; he was not particularly hopeful but got the interview. One of the first questions the interviewer asked him was, "Tell me something funny that happened on the train" in his current job. He told her a story and she was laughing so hard, she announced that she would like to hire him - would he be interested in the job? He asked for a couple of days to think about it. He explained his only hesitancy was the potential big pay cut – approximately fifty thousand dollars less than he was currently making at Amtrak.

He rarely ever asked Spirit for anything for himself, but decided he needed guidance.

Kevin pleaded with them, "Listen you need to help me with this. I will stay with Amtrak and never do another reading because I am getting too tired or I'll take the job with the airline and I'll continue doing readings. But you need to tell me which one. You need to give me a sign."

Kevin had a subscription to a magazine called "Airliners" which arrived in the mail that same day, approximately thirty minutes after his plea to Spirit. He opened it up and the magazine was bizarrely put together.

He described its confusing format, "On the first page you saw – it was actually page thirty-three. It was all writing except right in the middle was a picture of a Shuttle America plane taking off."

He laughed and thought, "This is my sign." He later called the magazine publisher to ask if anyone had noticed or reported this error and they responded they were not aware of this ever happening before, in the past or with this issue. He took the job.

Initially, times were tough financially for Kevin. In addition, Shuttle America was bought out within a few years by a new holding company. This meant that he would need to transfer to Pittsburgh. He decided that he did not want to relocate as the airline's longevity was also questionable and so, he was laid off. While he had a two-year waiting list as a medium in the past, business was slow due to a recession and an increase in other mediums in the area. The phone wasn't ringing. Kevin was depressed and broke. He missed flying.

"It's a job you can't describe. It's not even a job, it's a lifestyle."

He eventually was hired at another major airline out of Boston where he remains employed full-time today. But in the interim period of worrying about paying his bills, Kevin laughingly recalled looking up one day and saying to Spirit, "You sons of bitches, I am so broke and you told me to leave Amtrak and now I'm broke. I'm going away for two days, this telephone better ring when I come home."

When he returned home two days later, the phone rang. It was from a woman named Shirley who had invited him a few years back to do a reading with her husband Pat, a Boston radio host, at their home. Her husband Pat, originally a skeptic of mediums, had been so impressed with the reading that Kevin had given him, that he now had a business proposition for Kevin. This would turn out to be an ongoing working relationship with public medium events sponsored by the radio and TV station that Pat was affiliated with. It would continue into the next decade and to this day. It wouldn't get him rich by any means, but it has helped him to meet the expenses of his modest lifestyle. Pat's first reading, which convinced him of Kevin's ability, is described in Chapter 13.

Chapter 7: How Does the Process Work?

Kevin affectionately refers to the Spirits that he communicates with as "the Spooks." He is not being disrespectful and he is quite sure that they don't take offense at this term after all these years. He takes no credit himself in terms of having "a gift". He prefers to call his mediumship an "ability" vs. a gift. He credits Spirit [he typically uses the singular version of the word but meaning multiple people/spirits who want to work with him], without whom he would have no power to communicate with those who have passed.

One of the most challenging aspects of this project was to get Kevin to describe in detail how the process of mediumship works. He repeatedly said that he has no curiosity about the process itself. He knows it works for him, but he has no idea why or how.

"It's not what I think, it's what I know."

He has never questioned Spirit about why he was among those chosen with this ability and he has never asked Spirit to explain the afterlife to him.

While Kevin vividly recalls three Spirits at the bottom of his bed at the time when they first "spooked" him to go to unfoldment classes, they did not have specific features or names. But yet he can recognize them when they come to him. They look a bit like ethereal beings, not unlike what one might imagine a ghost would look like. He senses that they are the same three but perhaps there are a few others who regularly guide him since then, but he could not pin down a number or their names. He did say they are undoubtedly people who had once lived on earth but he had no idea who they were or when they had lived. It is these guides that he says help him during a reading – to help him connect with loved ones of the client that have passed. He may get messages during a reading in various forms from his regular Spirit mentors, a gatekeeper spirit or from those who have passed through the vibrations of the live person before him.

When pinned down to explain the process, he responded:

> "Well, it's a combination of stuff. First of all, I don't know exactly how it works, you know me with my lack of curiosity. It's not like I sit down with them and have a cup of coffee and I can interview them and they tell me how it all works. My understanding is that I have my guides; you have your guides. To some, it's called a guardian angel. My guides allow me to be able to do this. And I heard that there's a gatekeeper so when I'm reading you or anyone else, they allow certain spirit entities to come through to communicate with me. And so, it's all like a big chain, like a big telephone line."

There are many misconceptions out there about a medium's ability. Kevin described some of these:

> "Most people are wonderful but every once in a while, you get someone who's not cooperating. They don't want to accept what you said to them. It doesn't happen to me very often, thank God. But sometimes they are out there. They want to hear a certain thing, like, 'I'm thinking of a number – are you picking it up?' It just doesn't work that way. And some people don't understand that this is a very difficult process. It's not like I am having a two-way conversation with Spirit."

It has been well documented that a medium may use several different senses to communicate with Spirits. They may visualize a written or photographic type message or see an apparition (clairvoyance), hear a message (clairaudience) or feel or sense a message (clairsentience). In addition, Kevin and other mediums often have Spirit communication through olfaction, the sense of smell.

"Sometimes it's like looking at a movie. You see the movie in your mind, or sometimes you hear things," was one way Kevin described the process.

Brief examples of the various ways that Kevin has gathered information include the following vignettes.

During a reading with one client, Liv Ullmann, the Norwegian actress and film director, Kevin brought in her deceased father.

He told her that, "The letter that you were looking at in the past few days was from your father and it had Japanese writing on it."

Kevin has never studied the Japanese language and would normally not be able to distinguish Japanese writing from any other foreign language that also involves Kanji characters, which originated in the Chinese languages. Ms. Ullmann was born in Japan, but is not of Japanese descent. Kevin was not aware of that at the time but he had a vision, he could see the foreign characters in the letterhead and then sensed that they were Japanese words. Indeed, the client had been reading through her father's letters that very day that were sent from stationery with Japanese characters in the letterhead from a Japanese hotel that her father had stayed at years ago.

Kevin visited a friend of a friend one day in Boston for a reading and when he entered her apartment, he was struck with a vision of his own sister's childhood friend, Helene K., who had been murdered a few years ago. She had been killed by a random stranger who had followed her off a bus just a few days after her arrival in Colorado from Massachusetts. Kevin did not know the woman he was visiting in the North End of Boston but he clearly saw Helene K. from his sister's childhood who had lived in another part of Massachusetts.

"What the hell is Helene K. doing here?" he said to himself.

The woman who owned the apartment sensed something was wrong and asked him what he was seeing.

"Well, it's very bizarre, I'm seeing…. well, a friend my sister had in high school who was murdered in Colorado. She's standing in your living room."

"What was her name?"

"Well not that you would know her, but her name is Helene K."

"Oh my God that was my roommate in college!" the woman exclaimed.

When asked what does such an apparition look like, Kevin said, "You can see through them but they do look like a person." Helene's murder in the late 1970s or early 1980s was not solved for decades. Only a few years ago the murderer was captured after a tip led to a DNA test that was conducted on his beer glass at a public bar.

Another example of a vision was at a recent reading on Long Island at a woman's home.

Kevin was sitting in the kitchen with the woman giving her a reading from her loved ones that had passed. At one point said to her, "A man just walked by your window outside. He lived in this neighborhood and was murdered."

"Yes, three days ago a man was murdered in my neighborhood, a family member shot him," she responded.

In the course of one reading with a friend, Wendy Golini, Kevin sensed Spirit through clairaudience and clairvoyance. During the reading Kevin asked, "Did you go to Philadelphia recently or are you going to Philadelphia?"

She responded, "No."

"Are you sure? I see you in Philadelphia and hear you singing *Sweet Caroline*."

She replied again, "No, absolutely not!"

She had never been there and had no intention or reason for doing so anytime soon.

Kevin responded with his typical line, "Well, remember I said that."

Six months later, Wendy G. and her family went on a vacation to Puerto Rico. En route home, they had a connection in Philadelphia. It was April 15, 2013, the day of the Boston Marathon bombing. Their flight had a delay in Philadelphia until the Boston airport could re-open. She called Kevin several days later to share that indeed she had been cooped up in a bar at the Philadelphia airport when everyone spontaneously started singing *Sweet Caroline* in honor of all Bostonians and the Boston Red Sox. She joined in, not initially recalling his prior vision at the time. The Red Sox had beat the Tampa Bay Rays with the score of three to two earlier that day, an hour or so before the explosions. The *Sweet Caroline* song had long ago been unofficially adopted by the Red Sox as part of the eighth inning stretch period and typically it was sung in unison by all the fans in the ball park. So, in solidarity with all Bostonians, the delayed travelers in the Philly airport bar had erupted in this song on that day.

While Kevin does not consider himself a psychic per se, some of the messages he receives are difficult for him to interpret in terms of time, as noted – he may not know if the message is about something that has occurred or something that will happen in the future. But he had heard the song loud and clear and "saw" that she was in Philadelphia.

Similarly, at a group reading at Wendy G.'s home, Kevin brought in a woman's deceased father to her.

Right away, Kevin said to her, "Your father immediately started singing *Won't You Come Home, Bill Bailey.*"

The woman was amazed and almost "freaked out" as Kevin recalled.

She explained to him, "I just want you to know that my father was a tenor and in the 1950s there was this nationwide talent show. He and his friend won the talent show singing that song one year."

Wendy G. has hosted many medium reading parties with Kevin at her home over the twenty-five years that she has known him. She has witnessed Kevin giving readings countless times and has described what she has observed as his process. She has explained to people awaiting a reading at her home that there is often a sense of serendipity and/or a "tapestry" to his process. Serendipity, she describes, is often reflected in a person's readings over time; certain themes may emerge more than once. An example of this was related to the Sweet Caroline story. Not only did this message from Spirit arise as a result of the layover in Philadelphia that infamous day, the song had come up in the context of another reading by Kevin with her.

Several years prior to the Marathon bombing, she recalled a reading with Kevin:

> "He kept saying it [Sweet Caroline] to me and I was like, 'All right, I don't know what it means.' And then I took this job at an Irish bar and we did St. Patrick's Day. I loved the chef that we had. And probably the next morning we found out he had a massive heart attack and died that night. We were all very distraught and I remember his best friend said something and I kept hearing it [Sweet Caroline]. And he said it was his [the chef's] favorite song because it was his daughter's name. He used to sing it all the time."

Wendy G. also prepares the people who come to her home for readings that they might not hear what they want.

"They're looking for specific answers to things and nine out of ten times, it's a relationship question."

Witness to the World Beyond   43

But she explains that often the ones that have passed are parents who may want to talk about themselves a little bit first to give affirmation that it is truly them speaking through Kevin. And then they may or may not focus on what the adult child is going through at the time or respond to direct questions that the person being read may have. It is not set up as a question-and-answer period.

She also advises that, "Not all of them [the deceased] are skilled with that [communication with Kevin] as others might be."

She shared that after her brother died, he mainly communicated through songs to her which gave somewhat vague messages but since then "he has learned the language" and is much more specific with his communication through Kevin in more recent years.

Kevin typically asks the name of the person that has passed and where they lived and worked during a reading. He does not often ask their relationship right away as this often becomes clear to him soon enough. Generally, he does get a sense of how they died and sometimes this comes about by his feeling pain in the area himself. Other times, the deceased people will point to the general area that led to their death.

At a recent medium event in a community hall, where Kevin read a variety of random people who attended, he commented about a man who had passed to one of the participants, "Did he have throat problems? I feel pain in my throat."

When later asked what he meant by that, Kevin explained that he sometimes feels pain in the area where the person had medical issues or where the cause of death occurred. It used to be a rather challenging problem for him to feel this pain. He soon asked Spirit to stop that means of communication if possible and particularly, to dial down the intensity. The throat pain that he felt was minor that day and was an example of clairsentience.

An example of communication with Spirit through the sense of smell occurred during one reading with Alison Blake's husband, who hoped to have communication with his father who had just passed away less than a month ago.

The first thing Kevin said as both Alison and her husband sat down was, "I smell cigar smoke, does that make sense?"

They both said, "Yes."

"Well, I have a gentleman here and he liked to smoke cigars. I smell cigar smoke and he's with a friend of his who passed by falling off a roof."

Indeed, a close friend of the father was fixing the roof of a church when he fell to his death. And the father loved cigars.

"I mean how specific? – zap!" Alison exclaimed during her interview.

Another example of olfaction being involved in his communication with Spirit was a reading decades ago with Joe LeBlanc and his wife Marilyn about their beloved young adult son Joey, who had tragically died in a plane accident. Kevin identified the smell of Old Spice right away during one of the early readings. Indeed, Joe confirmed that his son always used Old Spice aftershave and deodorant. It was a minor detail among many to come that eased Joe and his wife's despair, knowing that Kevin was somehow in touch with their son's spirit. It brought enormous comfort to Joe and his wife during their time of profound grief.

During another reading with Joe and Marilyn, Kevin shared how he heard the word "Popeye." He didn't know or understand the context or what it meant but he told them, "Your son is telling me about Popeye. I heard him say the word "Popeye."

As it turned out, Joe had watched a movie the night before and there was a character called Popeye in the movie. His son was with him, Kevin told him. More stories from Joe, who has since become a dear friend of Kevin's, to follow in Chapters 9 and 16.

Frequently Kevin is asked, "How does it work in terms of walking down the street? Do you get vibes from every single person?"

As described in Chapter 4, early on Kevin "negotiated" with Spirit to not allow communication to come through unless he was purposefully reading someone. For the most part, he now "can shut it off like a light switch." Although at times he continues to get messages that he is not intentionally seeking out, they are typically harmless and not life-threatening ones. He referred to these episodes as warnings that come even though he thinks he has "turned it off". He laughingly referred to this as like an "emergency switch."

For example, he had been driving on the road one day and suddenly realized, "Oh my God, I need to stay way behind this car because she is about to have a car accident." And sure enough, "…a half mile up, she had a car accident."

Another example of a breakthrough of Spirit communication in his private life occurred as he was walking with a colleague in San Francisco during a layover.

As they passed by a store on their way back to their hotel, Kevin said to her, "You need to go into this store."

She asked, "Why?"

"I don't know but there's something in this store."

"Well, …what? What??"

"I don't know, there's just something for you in this store."

They both entered the store. Kevin waited by the front door as she took a left at the end of the L-shaped store toward the shoe department sign. She was gone for over fifteen minutes when he decided to try to find her. Soon he could hear her voice chatting away.

When she saw Kevin, she said, "Oh my God Kevin, you won't believe this! This is my niece from LA that I haven't seen in twenty years! She's here for the weekend."

Kevin knew that there was something for her in that store but he didn't know what and he didn't know how he knew that; it was just a sense he got.

"I just knew to tell her that. That is when you know you are really, really connected. And you know, that will happen quite a bit actually."

But for the most part, Kevin separates out his private life from his medium abilities.

"I want to be left alone from this. I don't want anything to do with it when I'm not doing it."

Kevin was not planning to do a reading as he entered a funeral home to attend the wake for the mother of his friend Vivian. But Spirit had a different plan. Several years prior, Vivian's mother had moved in with her and her family in the basement garden apartment. Her mother was aging and needed some help with shopping and meal preparation but for the most part, she was pretty independent. Her cause of death was recorded as a heart attack.

While at the services Kevin got several strong visions; he wasn't sure what the message meant but the woman's

Witness to the World Beyond   47

spirit was asking him to tell Vivian something at that moment. So, Kevin asked Vivian at the wake if he could briefly speak to her privately. They moved to a quiet corner of the funeral parlor.

"Your mom is showing me a couch," he said.

"Yeah, she died on the couch," Vivian replied.

Then he said, "Your mom is standing right here next to us and she's got a pillow in her hand. She's showing me a pillow. I don't know why your mother is showing me a pillow."

Vivian turned pale when he shared this vision and was speechless. His vision confirmed what she had suspected, that her mother had been suffocated. She had only shared her suspicions with her husband at that time. At the wake she did not tell Kevin what she feared had happened as he needed to get to the airport for work and she had to go back in the line to greet the large gathering of mourners at the wake. She knew she had to get through the wake and funeral before she could decide what action to take. Weeks later, she told Kevin the full story.

Vivian was the youngest of seven children with a span of fifteen years between her oldest sister and herself. That sister was more like a second mother to her all her life. A few days before their mother's death, the sister advised Vivian that she should not feel obligated to care for their mother, who had not always been a loving and tender mother to them as children. Vivian told her sister that it was all fine, their mother wasn't so dependent that it interfered with Vivian's ability to work. She also had older children who could check in on her mother periodically when she wasn't home.

"Well, I'm taking her out to the movies tomorrow and then I'm going to kill her," her sister told her.

Vivian just laughed the comment off.

The next day when Vivian came home from work, her sister greeted her in her home and said, "You need to get the kids out of the back yard NOW!"

"What? Why?" Vivian responded.

"I told you. I killed Mom."

Vivian was in total shock hearing this statement. She started screaming for her kids to come in through the porch door, not the basement, and felt paralyzed in a weird way. She could not bring herself to go downstairs and see her mother, knowing that she was just murdered and that she was too late to help her.

A day after the funeral and post funeral gathering at the house, Vivian shared what she suspected with her siblings; only one of them believed her. Her accusations caused a rift in the family and Vivian soon became estranged from most of her family for many years. Nonetheless she reported her suspicions to the police the next day. The body had already been cremated so there was no possibility of confirming her accusation. Her sister was "smart" and had seen to it that her mother was cremated immediately. The sister was eventually committed to a mental institution for an extended period but there was no criminal trial. Vivian explained that small towns like to handle these things "hush, hush" most likely because they hadn't followed their own protocol by simply believing that the elderly woman had died from a heart attack on the couch as reported by her daughter.

Ten years later, her now grown sons asked Vivian why she never talked about Nana and why she shuts down and goes silent when they mention her.

Then one son asked her, "Did Auntie kill Nana?"

And the other son admitted, "I think I saw Auntie do it."

Witness to the World Beyond   49

As it turned out, one of her sons had come in from the yard to use the basement bathroom that day and witnessed it. But as a young boy, he wasn't sure what he saw, particularly as the aunt invited him out for an ice cream the next day as she suspected he had seen something. When he mentioned he had been in the basement at that time, she explained that she was doing cardiopulmonary resuscitation (CPR) and was trying to save Nana. Although he was not totally reassured by his aunt, he never said anything more about it until a decade later when he told his mother. Indeed, he knew what he saw. And Kevin's communication with her Spirit the day of the wake was quite confirming as well.

Kevin's process in terms of individual readings includes a scheduled thirty-minute session conducted in a small office that he rents out periodically from a psychic, Darlyne Harff, who is a longtime friend of his. The office is decorated with all sorts of knickknacks that you might expect from a psychic's office. The lighting is dim, there are candles, spiritual pictures and crystals all around. At the time of the booking, an administrative assistant from this psychic's office instructs the person coming for a reading to bring pictures of loved ones that have passed. At one time Kevin had a two-year waiting list as he only does this part-time; more recently, he has been able to accommodate appointments within a few months of the booking.

Kevin encourages people to record the reading. He used to offer to record it himself on a small recorder and give the audiotape to the person. Now he suggests that they might want to record it using their phone. He initially asks to see the pictures they brought to the reading. And without any chitchat, he is off and running. Kevin often asks if they have pictures on their phone of their spouse, partner or children as the reading is in progress when he gets information about the living people from those who have passed.

Tori, a twenty-nine-year-old woman interviewed for this book, commented, "I was surprised he was so regular. I'm not sure if I was expecting a crystal ball or what. I was feeling very skeptical about everything initially but he just seemed down to earth and friendly. But he was also very like, okay let's get down to business, very matter of fact."

Several others who were interviewed commented on his unusual eye movements during the reading.

Jennifer, a sixty-year-old woman who was interviewed along with her husband Jake, said, "When Kevin is sitting in front of you and he's thinking about what he is going to say next, his eyes go back and forth like one thousand miles an hour, it's just so unnatural looking. I've never seen anything like it."

Others noted that Kevin looks not at you, but behind you, or sometimes he looks to his side and seems to be having a conversation with a spirit. Another observation mentioned by several interviewees was that it seemed odd that he didn't remember them at all from a prior reading, even from a year ago. Kevin did verify that he does so many readings over the course of a year, he rarely remembers people or the information he passed on to them.

When asked about how he manages his time during the readings, Kevin explained that he does not need to set a timer or look at his watch. He has an internal clock that tells him when the time is up.

In addition to scheduling private individual readings in an office, Kevin also does readings in private homes where the host coordinates a "medium party" and invites friends and family to come for individual briefer readings. Again, they are asked to bring pictures of loved ones that have passed. Each person is typically taken to a private room in the home for the reading, which lasts thirty minutes in length. After each reading, the participants generally share what they heard in their reading with each other. Some groups opt to have open readings in the group instead of private readings in the host's home. According to those interviewed for this book who have hosted medium parties, no one is ever disappointed.

As Lauren Torlone, a friend and client of Kevin's shared, "I feel like if this is a flop, I am so personally responsible for letting them down. But I've never had anybody that had a bad reading. So, you're putting yourself out there when you're the host. But everybody has always had a really good experience."

Three of her friends, also in their late thirties who participated in one home party, had all lost their mothers in their early twenties.

They all shared with Lauren, "I cannot believe that I literally talked to my mom."

Lauren further explained, "It was so validating for them to feel like their moms know them and their kids."

Indeed, many participants interviewed for this book concurred that Kevin could describe the personalities of their live loved ones, particularly children and grandchildren, with uncanny precision – through communication with their past loved ones.

Jennifer and her husband Jake interviewed together and agreed he had "pinpointed both of our kids to a T."

About their grown daughter, Kevin told them, "She has a good head on her shoulders, very level headed and works really hard. She is going to soon get a promotion." [which she did, soon thereafter].

Kevin also warned about her apartment, "It is a bad situation. She's going to be much happier in a new home. Better to get her out sooner than later."

They had already been worried about a possible fire in her apartment building and soon helped her move to another condo in the next town.

About their grown son, Kevin told them, "He's really high energy, he's a happy person and very environmentally plugged in." All of which was true.

"He was going green before anyone was green," Jennifer shared.

Jenn and Jake also recalled that her deceased mother had told them through Kevin, "Jimmy's [their son] eyes are going to be ok."

At the time, that had no meaning. Ten years later, he developed an eye condition that required steroids. He was hesitant to take the medication because of possible added side effects.

Jenn noted, "It's one of his best features. He has incredibly gorgeous eyes."

"It should be mentioned, he is a handsome boy and he's really vain and so his eyes were important to him," her husband replied with a laugh.

Their son did not develop the side effect from the medication. They are quite convinced that her mother's earlier message was referring to this situation years later. Kevin also commented that their son worked for a "democratic figure"; he had interned with John Kerry, the former MA senator.

Patricia, a retired nurse who lives with her daughter and her two young children, also agreed that his description of her grandchildren was uncanny. She showed him a picture with all four of her grandchildren.

He immediately pointed to the two that lived with her and asked, "Do you take care of them all the time?"

He pointed to one that he said was "really affectionate" and another that "mark my words, this one's a little trouble."

She laughed as she recalled this, "He is at the age that he's constant, like you have to be with him because he will get into everything."

But Kevin reassured her that, "They are all good. I don't see any real problems with any of them."

He asked, "Has the younger one [age one and a half] been really quiet lately?"

"Well, he hasn't really started talking," she replied.

Kevin noted his parents are worried about it since they are comparing him to the others.

"But there's nothing wrong with him, as long as he is happy."

All of these insights came from Patricia's deceased father who described them each to Kevin and who also gave Patricia credit for raising her own children and the grandchildren so well.

At another reading during a house party event, Kevin recalled:

> "One woman came in and sat down. She had a picture of her mother. And I said that this woman was stabbed multiple times and you were on your way to visit her when it happened, right around

Christmas. You were on your way to Vermont and she was stabbed and robbed."

Kevin described that the woman tearfully exclaimed that his reading was correct about the circumstances regarding her mother's death. Almost everyone in attendance cried at some point that evening.

Many apologized for crying but he responded, "I don't care if you are crying. As a matter of fact, it makes it easier to read you if you are crying or if you laugh. It raises the vibration so it makes it easier to communicate."

He later clarified in our interview together by adding that, while strong emotions can facilitate the process of reading someone, "If you don't want to be read, you can't be read. If you put that wall up, I can't get through that wall."

Kevin went to a client's home per her request once in the Magnolia section of Gloucester, MA. He commented on the lovely home. It was an open concept ranch with a fireplace in the middle of the main room. It was tastefully decorated with a warm and welcome feeling upon entry.

"What a beautiful home you have," Kevin commented.

"Don't you remember me?" the woman asked.

Initially he did not recall meeting her until she reminded him that several years prior, Kevin had told her at a medium house party, "You have a lovely home."

"Oh, I hate it, it needs so much work," the woman responded at the time.

"Don't worry, you're going to be able to do all the work," Kevin predicted.

"Nope, we don't have the money."

"No, you're going to have the money, a car is going to drive right through your kitchen."

Several weeks later, the brakes of a neighbor's parked car failed and the car rolled right through her kitchen. No one was injured. She was thrilled to be able to redecorate it with the insurance money.

At times the spirits are in competition with each other and the messages can get crossed. For example, Alan, a data engineer in his forties, was being read one time and Kevin immediately picked up that his sister had died of a heroin overdose as Kevin was being shown track marks.

That was correct but he then asked Alan, "Were you just standing out at your stoop and wondering about putting a jack-o-lantern there?"

It was Halloween time but Alan denied that he had contemplated such decorations.

Next, Kevin asked him, "Well were you just at your father's grave and pulling out weeds there?"

Again, this didn't make any sense to Alan. He went home and told his partner Mark about the things that were on target from Kevin's reading and those that made no sense. Mark told him – it must have been his own grandfather, who was like a father to him, that came through at that point. Mark explained to Alan that he had been with his family the weekend prior and had specifically thought about putting a decorated pumpkin on the porch stoop and he had also spent several hours at his grandfather's grave pulling out weeds. Since then, Alan commented that it has happened more than that one time that his own father and Mark's grandfather "sort of battle for the spotlight," during his readings with Kevin.

Alan also shared the story of a FaceTime reading by Kevin to his partner and his partner's grandmother. Kevin told them both that he could see the grandmother's deceased husband, Mark's grandfather, holding up something that looked like a waffle.

"Why is he showing me this?" Kevin asked them.

Neither of them had a clue what he was talking about and assumed he just wasn't getting the signals right.

But Alan then blurted out, "Those were his pizzelles!"

Alan explained in the interview that pizzelles are waffle-like cookies that were Mark's grandfather's specialty. He made them every Christmas.

Alan concluded, "It was his thing! It goes to show how much of a mental block people can have while sitting at a reading. The aha moments often come afterwards or from someone not in the spotlight."

A cross of spirit messages also occurred during one of Paul M.'s readings with Kevin. While Kevin was sharing messages from Paul's brother Michael, who had committed suicide, he veered off into a few messages that didn't make sense.

"There was something in the blood," Kevin said.

Paul recalled during his interview that he thought that was not something related to his brother.

"Wait a minute, I think you've got someone else there too," Paul recalled telling Kevin.

Kevin asked, "Is he sarcastic?"

Paul answered, "Yes."

And then Paul realized that it was his friend Adam who had died from AIDS in the 1990s trying to connect with him.

Kevin then told him, "He just wants to tell you, Nieman Marcus."

"Slam two!" Paul exclaimed in his interview - referring to two very specific messages from past loved ones, his brother and now his friend Adam. Adam had worked on Newbury St. in Boston among the fancy clothing stores and used to take Paul shopping in the high-end places, including Nieman Marcus.

In addition to reading people individually and doing home readings, Kevin also on occasion does a "medium show" at a restaurant venue or community center site. This may involve from forty to one hundred plus people in attendance; most come in the hope that they will be chosen for a reading. Others come to support a friend or simply to observe and watch "the show." Typically, this will include food served during the intermission or a buffet dinner before the show. On average, sixteen people will get chosen for brief, seven-to-ten-minute readings during this event – all of which are done in public. Each person interested in a reading is asked to initially leave just one picture of a deceased loved one face up on a front table.

At the beginning of these programs, Kevin walks slowly around the table and picks one picture up at a time. He holds the picture up while he describes it and the corresponding participant who brought the picture is asked to stand up. Again, he asks just a few general questions at the outset, such as in what city did the deceased person live and work and where does the standing person live and work now. After about seven to ten minutes, he moves on to another picture that he picks seemingly at random, but as he explains, he picks pictures that he is drawn to for reasons that he cannot explain other than Spirit has guided him. And he then proceeds to tell what messages he is getting from the deceased person. If he makes a declarative statement about them or the person standing, he follows up with, "Do you understand?" seeking brief affirmation.

When Kevin doesn't get a confirmation that his comments are understood, Kevin doesn't retract what he said, he simply says, "Remember that I said that."

Alison Blake shared in her interview an encounter that she witnessed that touched her during a reading in a public show.

> "He [Kevin] picked up a picture and it was a younger guy, maybe forty. He said, 'This guy passed away very recently. He was a big football fan and he loved the Patriots.' The woman [wife]…started bawling because everything he's saying is just so true. Kevin said, 'He had a special chair, a recliner that he used to watch the game in.' She replied, 'Yes, yes!' Kevin continued, 'Nobody in the family wants to sit in that chair, do they?' And she was like, 'No, no, no…no one will sit in that.' Kevin told her that, 'his love for the Patriots was really great, he was more than just a regular fan.' And the woman acknowledged that yes, they had buried him in his Patriots jersey."

Scott Whitley, a TV and radio personality who often hosts some of Kevin's public dinner shows, shared his own observations:

> "If Kevin couldn't do it, I wouldn't be involved because I have my own reputation to protect. With

Kevin…it's just a guarantee. And you can see people when they get up and they're being read, some of them, you know, really start to shake. It's just amazing. By the end of the reading, he really puts them at ease because they are getting something that they maybe felt they have missed or lost or didn't get to say or experience. It gives them closure or hope. I think that is reassuring to a lot of people."

One of Scott's observations at an event that he sponsored involved the reading of a young woman in her thirties, a school teacher, whose husband had recently passed away.

Kevin told her, "You're going to go outside and going to be on this hill overlooking water. When you see cardinals, he's going to be with you."

Scott happened to be sitting near her and observed her pull out her phone and show people around her a picture from that very morning.

"She was sitting on a perch overlooking a huge lake and there were hundreds of cardinals all around her," Scott recalled.

Scott mentioned during his interview that people in attendance at these shows commonly ask him, "Did Kevin get a list of the attendants in advance?"

He assures them that Kevin has never asked for that and that Kevin has never received any information about those who had registered for the event.

At one of the Whitley sponsored medium dinner shows, Kevin read a man named Carl who was a friend of Scott's father.

"Who is an attorney?" Kevin asked.

"I am an attorney," Carl responded.

"Do you live or work near Newburyport High School?"

"Yes, I have an office near there."

"And there's a house in Maine that the steps were ripped out of?"

"We did that this weekend, just yesterday as a matter of fact."

"Everybody refers to your mother as St. Mary."

Carl's eyes teared up after this remark. Kevin told him that she sent her blessings as his time was about up. Soon afterwards it was time for a short break in the readings.

During the break Pat Whitley came over and told Kevin, "Carl has something to share with you but he wants to share it with the whole audience after the break is over."

Kevin agreed that would be fine. Carl stood up before the audience who had just heard his public reading at the restaurant show and shared:

> "I want you to know that my mother's name is Mary F. She was a crossing guard in Melrose and many years ago, a car went out of control while she was working. It was about to hit several children but she was able to push them out of the way. She was killed in the process. It happened at St. Mary's School and her funeral was at St. Mary's Church. The priest said at her funeral, 'This parish was named one hundred years too early. It should be named after the real St. Mary, Mary F.' The church has a picture of her with the name St. Mary under it on proud display."

Aprile Albertelli is a woman from Medway, MA, in her early sixties. She came with a friend to one of the Scott

Witness to the World Beyond   61

Whitley sponsored dinner shows held at a Chinese restaurant in North Andover, MA. She was hoping to be one of the lucky ones to get chosen for a reading as her beloved mother had died two years prior. After Kevin chose her mother's picture and showed the crowd, Aprile excitedly stood up to claim it was hers. Her friend taped the reading and shared it with the author who later transcribed it with Aprile's permission along with permission to use her real name.

> Kevin: Hi there, and your name is…?
> Aprile: Aprile
> Kevin: Aprile, ok. And what town do you live in?
> Aprile: Medway.
> Kevin: And her name is?
> Aprile: Elaine.
> Kevin: And what town did she live?
> Aprile: Franklin
> Kevin: And that's in that area too, isn't it?
> Aprile: Yes.
> Kevin: This was your mom?
> Aprile: Yes.
> Kevin: Can I ask you something? It doesn't have to be her. But have you anybody that has a problem with her head? Could be a brain tumor or an aneurysm or a stroke? And I'd feel better with a female than a male.
> Aprile: Recently my dad told me that a friend of theirs from Florida [a woman] recently just had a stroke.
> Kevin: That's what it is, would have been only a week or two ago.
> Aprile: It was.
> Kevin: You look a little bit like your mom. I just wanted you to know that she was there as that was being discussed. And it's funny too because when she was ill and

wasn't feeling well, she didn't want everybody to know about it, do you understand?

Aprile: Yes.

Kevin: And I don't know if she had cancer or not but if she didn't, she had more than one problem in her body. One of the two, you understand?

Aprile: Yes, she did.

Kevin: And I don't know why but my midsection is bothering me. Quite a bit. You understand?

Aprile: Yes.

Kevin: And she was in a lot of pain but she downplayed that, you understand?

Aprile: Yeah.

Kevin: And I feel that you were the one that would drive her around, you understand?

Aprile: Mmm hmm [nods yes].

Kevin: And she really appreciated that. And what town does your dad live in now?

Aprile: Franklin.

Kevin: Franklin, OK. He was…he really, didn't… didn't handle this well, you understand?

Aprile: Yes.

Kevin: You might have other siblings as well but I'm talking about that you stepped up to the plate, you understand?

Aprile: Yup.

Kevin: Because she's saying in a kind way… but she's saying that he was kind of useless? [audience laughter]. You understand?

Aprile: Yes.

Kevin: And then sometimes you'd take her to lunch after certain appointments, you understand?

Aprile: Yes.

Witness to the World Beyond   63

Kevin: And I want you to know that she really cherished that, you understand?

Aprile: Yes.

Kevin: Can I ask you something? Do you have a car that has a headlight out? Or a brake light?

Aprile: Recently I was told that my license plate light was out.

Kevin: Your license plate? That's fine, that's close enough [small audience laughter]. And I just want you to know that she knows all about that. [laughter].

Aprile: Thanks mom! [more audience laughter].

Kevin: And do you happen to have a shade in your house that doesn't come down properly?

Aprile: Yes.

Kevin: You were screwing around with it the other day, you understand? [laughter].

Aprile: Yeah.

Kevin: She was right there behind you when you were doing that. You even said, 'this GD thing!' [laughter].

Aprile: I did!

Kevin: I just heard her say, 'that's my girl,' you understand? [audience sighs "aww" with small laugh]. Do you know anybody who could have worked in a bank or something with numbers?

Aprile: No.

Kevin: She did know someone? I don't even know if this a person, but I'm being shown numbers.

Aprile: Just numbers?

Kevin: Yeah, but it seems like it could be a bank or even something about mortgages. I just don't know what it is.

Aprile: Okay.

Kevin: Did you know anybody?

Aprile: My dad just finished a deal where somebody owed him money.

Kevin: Can I ask you something? Did he have to use somebody from the outside to help him with that?

Aprile: Yes.

Kevin: That's what it is. And it wasn't that long ago.

Aprile: Yes.

Kevin: Ok and your mom knew all about that. And I just feel – was somebody trying to take advantage of him?

Aprile: Yes.

Kevin: But he's not the type of person that is good at putting his foot down, do you understand?

Aprile: Correct

Kevin: Somebody else was pushing him – you have to get help. You understand?

Aprile: Yup.

Kevin: And it doesn't have to be you, but somebody was trying to push the thought out to your mother that she had to help him with that, you understand?

Aprile: Yeah, we're always talking to her [laughs]. 'Dad needs help!' [audience laughter].

Kevin: And I have to be honest with you. He's like the absent minded professor, you understand? [laughter]. He means well but she was always the one that had to push him and everything else, you understand?

Aprile: Oh yes.

Kevin: And is he on some medications that he is not taking?

Aprile: Yes.

Kevin: You're going to have to keep an eye on that. Because that medication means all the difference in the world for him.

Aprile: It was glaucoma. He wasn't taking the medication. He didn't think he had to. We said, 'Do you want to go blind?'

Kevin: So, you are going to have to keep an eye on that because he is going to do that again. And she's so cute she just said, 'Just do it for me.' And she wants to thank you. I feel you live closer than the other siblings to your father.

Aprile: I am.

Kevin: So, it is on your shoulders. But your father is a nice man. You understand?

Aprile: Yeah, he's a sweetheart.

Kevin: And he appreciates it when you just sit there and watch TV with him. You understand?

Aprile: Yup.

Kevin: And you say you're there to visit but you are really checking up on him. Can I ask a question? Was anybody in the family in the navy?

Aprile: Yes…. ummm my father's brother.

Kevin: He's in spirit?

Aprile: Yes, my father's brother.

Kevin: Because there's a gentleman here, he's in a Navy uniform and he just wants to say hello.

Aprile: Okay.

Kevin: And you're going to have a problem with your leg or your knee, if you haven't already. You understand?

April: I sure do [laughter].

Kevin: And you were in the kitchen or the dining room recently and you said, "I hope I don't have to have a knee replacement." You understand?

Aprile: Yup.

Kevin: That was, those were your exact words., the conversation was like in the last week or two. And I'm not saying you have to …but there is an issue. You are walking, but you are supposed to be walking more than you do. And you haven't been. You understand?

Aprile: Right.

Kevin: Somebody said, "Well just walk around the block a few times." That's what they said to you and you still aren't doing it [much laughter from audience]. Don't you love it when your mother scolds you? [more laughter].

Aprile: Jeez Louise! [laughs].

Kevin: No, you can't hide from that.

Aprile: No!

Kevin: Anyway, you haven't been good about that.

Aprile: I have not.

Kevin: And when you went to the doctor, you were getting really testy about it, you understand?

Aprile: I do.

Kevin: Because you are your own worst enemy. 'You take after me,' she says. She has a mind of her own. But you do too [laughter]. But you are going to have to or otherwise there's going to be some problems. Okay?

Aprile: Okay.

Kevin: I know it's really only one knee. But you were thinking, "I'll have one knee done and then next thing I'll need the other one done." Understand?

Aprile: Mmm hmm [nods yes].

Kevin: So, you are just trying to avoid that. So just listen to her, listen to your mother. And with that I'll leave her blessing [audience claps; Aprile is smiling with tears in her eyes].

At another public event in a community hall in Gloucester MA, Kevin gave nineteen readings over a two-hour period with a fifteen-minute intermission break, an average of a

Witness to the World Beyond   67

seven and a half minute reading for each person chosen. The majority of readings were with women in the audience, two were with men. Over half were from Gloucester themselves, the remainder from a smattering of MA cities and towns. All the names are aliases, but to get a feeling of the rather specific evidence Kevin can give in a rapid-fire session, here is a sampling of notes taken from the event; it was not recorded.

Melinda was a young girl from the Boston area who had come with a girlfriend. She had brought a picture of an older woman, who also lived in her same city.

Kevin: Was she your grandmother?
Melinda: Yes.
Kevin: Did anyone in the family have an abortion or miscarriage? They look the same to me.
Melinda: Yes, my mother.
Kevin: The child is with your grandmother. Was this your mother, - life is not good, on welfare, not coming out of the house, watching TV all day, in a depression?
Melinda: Yes
Kevin: How old are you?
Melinda: Twenty
Kevin: Did you just barely finish high school?
Melinda: Yes.
Kevin: You ARE intelligent! You might go to trade school. You ARE capable! There's nothing wrong with you. The garbage in your family has affected you. Where is your dad?
Melinda: He lives far away.
Kevin: You never saw him often?
Melinda: Yes

Kevin: Your grandmother will push you. Did you ever get your driver's license?

Melinda: Just two days ago.

Kevin: You don't like to drive?

Melinda: No, I don't.

Kevin: You have so much anxiety. You will never be the belle of the ball but 'enough is enough' says your grandmother. So much unhappiness. Do you have friends that dress in goth?

Melinda: I have some friends like that.

Kevin: You are all like the island of misfit toys [small laughter from audience]- but you are NOT a misfit! You could be good as a chef. You didn't want to be near people in high school. Your grandmother says, 'You need to learn to live your life.' She sends her love and blessing. [Many people in the audience were teary eyed, along with Melinda at the end.]

Craig, a distinguished looking man in his sixties stood up when his wife Sofia's picture was chosen. After asking where they both lived and the city/town where they worked (Gloucester on all accounts), Kevin began with:

Kevin: Do you have a problem with your shoulder and neck?

Craig: Yes.

Kevin: You need to see a doctor about that. Who had cancer?

Craig: She did.

Kevin: Who has a problem now with their midsection?

Craig: Her daughter.

Kevin: She [Sofia] always downplayed how she felt.

Witness to the World Beyond   69

Craig: Yes.

Kevin: But your being there was enough. Is there a car on the property all the time?

Craig: Well, no but there is a truck.

Kevin: Well, I should have said vehicle [audience laughs]. She is there all the time. Is it a tow truck?

Craig: Yes.

Kevin: Someone is buying a new car soon.

Craig: Yes.

Kevin: You thought you would be helpless without her but you aren't.

Craig: Yes.

Kevin: Is her daughter going to Florida?

Craig: Yes.

Kevin: Do you need a new couch?

Craig: Yes [audience laughter].

Kevin: On Saturdays from seven to eight pm you miss her the most. She urges you to walk. You get up at 4:00 – 4:30 am, she's always there. Did you put up new window treatments or something new on the wall?

Craig: Yes.

Kevin: She sends her love and blessings.

Judy was a middle-aged attractive woman who lived and worked in different MA towns outside of Gloucester. She brought a picture of an older man who lived in Gloucester and worked "in many places."

Kevin: Was he your dad?

Judy: Yes.

Kevin: Who boxed? It wasn't your father.

Judy: My brother.

Kevin: Is he ok?

Judy: I don't know.

Kevin: When did your dad pass?

Judy: A few years ago.

Kevin: You had a lot of dysfunction in your family. Do you have anger issues? Are you still pissed?

Judy: Yes.

Kevin: I did come from that as well; it was overwhelming at times. He was a disappointment to you, not exactly the father of the year.

Judy: Yes [she is crying now].

Kevin: You asked, 'How could you do this to me?' But you are a survivor. He apologizes. Was he involved with a younger woman?

Judy: Yes.

Kevin: People joked that she was his daughter.

Judy: Yes.

Kevin: He says, 'I made a lot of mistakes.' Your mother passed too?

Judy: Yes.

Kevin: She was a mother to a lot of people? She had four kids but was a mother to others as well.

Judy: Yes.

Kevin: Did you see a bean bag chair recently?

Judy: I don't know.

Kevin: Well, remember I said that. Who rides a motorcycle?

Judy: My husband.

Kevin: Your mother says, 'I love her and will do what I can for her but... you have a way of picking them too.' He [her father] wants better for you than what he was able to give you. Who got a tattoo?

Judy: I have some.

Kevin: You have much unhappiness living on the North Shore?

Judy: Yes.

Kevin: Is there a problem with your garage?

Judy: Yes.

Kevin: You can overcome your problems. You have depression?

Judy: Yes.

Kevin: You are on the wrong medication or wrong doses. You are trying to get rid of your past. You can't do that. They both send their love and blessings.

Doug was a bit of a burly man in great shape, who lived a few towns over from Gloucester. He appeared to be in his early sixties and came with his wife. The picture he had left on the table was his best friend Robbie, holding a fishing rod in front of his truck. Robbie had lived and worked in VT most recently before his unexpected death.

Kevin: I see a very rural living situation, of course Vermont is quite rural. I see a pick-up truck and a dirt drive.

Doug: Yes.

Kevin: How old was he when he passed?

Doug: Sixty.

Kevin: Was he living a reclusive life when he passed?

Doug: Yes and no.

Kevin: But he didn't have a lot of contact with his family, right?

Doug: Yes, he did.

Kevin: Are you sure?

Doug: Well, he had one brother he had problems with.

Kevin: Did you go there a lot?

Doug: No.

Kevin: Were there plastic coverings on the wall?

Doug: No.

Kevin: Was his digestion, ok?

Doug: No.

Kevin: Did you recently look at a picture of him flipping the bird?

Doug: Yes.

Kevin: He knew how to have fun, didn't he?

Doug: Yes.

Kevin: He enjoyed alcohol but wasn't an alcoholic.

Doug: Yes.

Kevin: But one of you did have alcohol poisoning in the past, right?

Doug: Yes, we all did at one time [audience laughter].

Kevin: He was a really good guy. Who was it who had a gambling problem?

Doug: One of the guys in the group.

Kevin: Was there a boat that sank or disappeared in the water?

Doug: Not that I remember, but maybe a canoe.

Kevin: It was near you two or close to you. Now I see an intersection with four corners near a Dunkin Donuts. Did you go through a red light there recently?

Doug: I go through red lights there every day [audience laughter].

Kevin: He says to be careful there. He liked his beer. Things aren't the same without him, right?

Doug: Yes.

Kevin: Where you spent time with him, there was a mishmash of furniture?

Doug: No, his house wasn't like that. Oh…[pauses] but he owned an inn and we did spend a lot of time there. Everything was bought at a yard sale [audience laughter].

Kevin: He never wanted to grow up.

Doug: I still don't know what I want to be when I grow up [audience laughter].

Witness to the World Beyond   73

Kevin: Who was the electrician?

Doug: I don't know.

Kevin: You will hear about this. Remember I said this. Do you know some cops or firefighters?

Doug: I know them all in town [audience laughter].

Kevin: You could visit Robbie at any time unannounced.

Doug: Yes, he sometimes found me naked on his couch in the morning [audience laughter].

Kevin: It is such a disappointment to you; you've never had the same fun since he died. The crowd has dissipated.

Doug: Yes.

Kevin: He says to 'Give 'em hell.' And that you will always find fun.

[Doug was speechless at the end, with tears running down his face.]

Kevin was asked after that public medium event about potential concerns about such private information at times being shared in a room full of strangers. Could identifying such things as mental health issues past and present in an open forum cause harm to the people being read? He responded that this has never been an issue in over twenty-five years that he had done such events. He has come to trust Spirit with the amount and type of information he is given during a reading – that what comes through is what the person can handle.

Common questions that people often pose to Kevin relating to the possibility of a spiritual life after death include: Is there a God? What does the afterlife look like?

What are the spirits doing? Is there a heaven and hell? Is there such a thing as reincarnation?

Kevin generally responds that he does not ask such questions of Spirit. He denies curiosity about the topic despite his uncommon ability. While he is skeptical about many modern-day mediums who claim to have these answers, he did believe firmly in one of his earlier teachers, Gladys Worsencroft, as well as the former nationally known political reporter, syndicated columnist and author who later in life wrote of her own rather unique medium capabilities, Ruth S. Montgomery.

Gladys W. told him the story once of her "visit" to the afterlife. Her guides told her one night that they were taking her over to the other side and to be prepared.

"Just lie down in the bed like you normally do and we'll come for you," Kevin recalled her describing their directions to him.

She told Kevin that, "they lifted her right off the bed and were going for the wall."

She had the sensation of crashing into the wall of her bedroom and was then "over the other side." She visited with two people who had passed that used to live locally in two North Shore towns in MA, neither of whom she had ever met. One was a young woman who had worked at a local former shoe factory. She was wearing a bracelet that her mother had given her. When Gladys later went to find the mother to give her a message from her daughter, the mother confirmed the bracelet had been a gift. Gladys also described to Kevin her observation that people can recreate their own homes on the other side.

The other man she "visited" on the other side had a message for his wife. His last name was King and he asked Gladys to tell his living wife that, "The King will always be waiting for his Queen."

Witness to the World Beyond   75

When she found Mrs. King and told her this, her response was, "Oh my God, he used to say that to me all the time when he was dying. The king will always wait for his queen."

Kevin's assessment of these events was that they were true.

As he explained, "To be honest with you, I don't think I would trust anyone else; I do trust her because she was an incredible medium."

Kevin also commented that he does not watch TV shows, documentaries or movies about mediumship and rarely has read about them, other than being introduced to Ruth Montgomery's work years ago which he found credible.

"She was a good author who wrote a series of books. I did like her. Her books, *Search for Truth* and *A World Beyond*, are on Kindle."

Kevin does not describe himself as a religious or spiritual person per se, but he does believe in a God.

He rarely attends any church services these days. In terms of traveling to "spiritual" places, such as Sedona, Arizona, "That stuff bores the living hell out of me."

One of his friends and clients, Lauren Torlone, an accomplished writer and educator, asked him about hell, "Is there a place for bad people? What about Hitler?"

She recalled that his response was, "No. Everybody finds their own level of like persons. If you're a bad person on earth, you're going to end up with other bad people. You're not sent to burn in hell but you are with all the same type of people as you. My impression is that they don't really care that they're not in the most amazing part because they are not actually good people."

76   Barbara Ellen Mawn

Although he tries to get Lauren off the topic, she noted with a smile, she sometimes persists.

"What does a dead person think about the pandemic?" she once asked.

He responded, "It's not a thing. You have to understand that this is the arc of time, you know? This [the pandemic] is a very small thing; they don't care about these things in time."

In terms of reincarnation, Kevin noted, "The one thing that I don't get into is reincarnation because it can't be proven. I'd rather tell you about somebody you know – that you were in your kitchen yesterday and this is the conversation you had."

He also acknowledged that he's never tried to connect with someone that had passed and been told… "sorry, they've gone into another life. It makes you wonder about that. Reincarnation can't be scientifically proven but mediumship has been proven."

And yet, Lauren Torlone, who has had approximately six readings over the past ten years, shared:

> "A common thing he always said to me which I do connect with even though I am not into past lives is 'I always see looming or dressmaking or doll making connected to you in a past time. You have some sort of colonial history.' And I definitely have felt that since I was a little kid, my family would joke with me when we would have colonial day. Literally from a young age, I was like - *I've lived this life before, one hundred percent!*"

Lauren clarified that Kevin never used the term "previous life" or "reincarnation" - just that there was "a

Witness to the World Beyond   77

connection" to colonial times that came up in several readings.

While Kevin generally prefers to use pictures of loved ones during a reading, he can connect to Spirits without pictures as well. He mentioned, "I found a dead body using the phone once." And so, he explained:

"I got a call one day. I was in Washington actually, working for Amtrak. It was like nine or ten o'clock at night.

Karina [his former friend] called and said, 'Kevin there's a girl that jumped off a bridge and killed herself. They can't find the body.'

I usually asked for somebody's name but this time I didn't. I said, 'Well who would Emma be?' Because I could see this older woman named Emma.

She said, 'Well that's the name of the girl who killed herself.'

I said, 'Well, that's not making sense because this woman looks very old.'

She said, 'Oh, well her grandmother's name was Emma.'

I said, 'Ah that's the one.'

When the police went to the home of Emma's parents to tell them, the grandfather, the husband of the deceased grandmother Emma, was there and he immediately passed of a heart attack after the news. So, they had two deaths in one night.

So anyhow, Karina explained, 'They can't find the body and they've been looking and looking.'

I said, 'They are on the wrong side of the bridge; they shouldn't be over there. They need to be on the side toward the railroad tracks.'

'Are they going to find the body?'

'Yeah.'

I looked over at this woman Emma and she held out all five fingers of her hand. I generally never get things like this.

I said, 'Well, within a five they will find her.'

Karina asked, 'Well, within five hours? Five days?'

I looked at Emma again and she very forcefully held up her hand a second time. I thought I don't want to screw with this woman, she doesn't seem too happy now.

'Just remember that -within a five. And she will be found by a guy named Barry, who's in a boat.'

Well, I didn't hear anything about it afterwards until weeks later. One night, Karina joined the unfoldment class I was taking and she joined my circle. She shared with the group the story and then ended with - I just want you to know they found her body on the first day of the fifth week by a guy named Barry who was clamming in a boat."

Emma was also found on the side of the bridge that Kevin had specified. The story of Emma would come up again during a future reading with another woman unexpectedly, more to follow in Chapter 14.

Chapter 8: Living Life on His Own Terms

Kevin continues to work full-time as a flight attendant and schedules individual readings, house parties, dinner shows or community medium events on a part-time basis. He strives for a balanced life with his full-time commitment to his passion, flying, and part-time devotion to his other calling, mediumship. He has many dear life-long friendships, a few that have resulted from his readings, but none of his close friends are mediums themselves. He is happily single, prefers to live alone, a self-proclaimed introvert who is comfortable with his own company as well as the occasional company of his family and close friends.

When asked if he had children, he responded with a smile, "No, no, just a plant."

Kevin is close to two of his sisters and is a beloved uncle. His nieces think he is "the coolest and funniest uncle" according to his sister Kathy. His sister Kathy de Lacy, who is three years younger than Kevin, recalled that the four siblings all had their own individual interests growing up and weren't particularly close.

She acknowledged the "difficult circumstances" of their childhood years but noted that Kevin has "never played the victim...that was not going to determine our future."

Looking back on his childhood, Kathy thought that they all attributed his occasional unexplained behaviors as being related to having "invisible friends," a common experience for many children.

His sister Kathy commented that as an adult, "There are so many other layers to him [beyond being a medium]. Kevin is very bright; he probably reads more than any person I know. He loves books."

She also acknowledged that he is somewhat reserved and not self-promoting. Kathy described him as a very talented clarinet player "...with a love of music and a vast collection of music." She described him as, "quiet...unless he knows you." She mentioned that he "has a dry wit and is just very funny," and has observed him working his dry sense of humor into his shows as well.

Kathy also noted that "as a family, we don't spend too much time on the subject of mediumship." She has observed his ability at shows and has attended his house parties. She has witnessed the emotions and sometimes the shock on the faces of those who are being read. But after the shock wears off, she notices "a smile on their face and a sense of peace."

"He's a fascinating person to be with. I can't begin to tell you how proud of him I am. He's doing his life on his terms. And that, I think, is pretty amazing."

And yet his sister acknowledged that, "I don't always feel like he's totally comfortable with his ability. I think sometimes, he might say it's somewhat of a burden. He has to really set boundaries with people."

Kevin prefers to conduct readings in person, whether it be with an individual in a private or group setting. He also mentioned during one of his interviews that he is capable of conducting readings over the phone but is not interested in using Zoom or other video applications. He does phone readings only rarely however, because it has at times led to people harassing him for "urgent" (to them) readings. As it is, he often keeps his phone off much of the time to avoid such a problem.

He explained, "I like to have a normal life. I know when I'm going to the office to do readings, I get myself psyched for the day. I know if I'm going to have ten people, it's going to be busy. But it seems to be an invasion when people call and they want it over the phone. So especially if someone is local, I ask them to go to the office. Trust me when I say that some people bother you."

Sometimes Kevin calls his ability "a curse." The key is to control the ability and manage his time which he has worked on for his entire adult life. At this point, he is comfortable with his relationship with Spirit. He described the two-way process:

> "Spirit learns to work with you the way you want it. I know there was a medium who claimed that if she didn't wear a headphone and baseball cap when she flies, Spirit won't leave her alone [on the plane]. You've got to be kidding me. You claim you are such a great medium and you can't control that? They will work with you the way that you want to work. You know technically even though they are giving the message, you can think they are in charge. But really, they are not. I'm in charge. And if I didn't want to work with them, I would just walk away. So, they

want to work with you and so they are going to do it the way that is acceptable to you."

When asked about his "success rate" by his friend and client Lauren Torlone, Kevin responded that it is "...basically one hundred percent." In over twenty-five years of conducting thousands of readings, the friend Darlene, whose office he rents, reported that only two to three complaints have come to her. None of these were a major concern; they were related to unsatisfied customers who wanted something more out of the experience or something different told to them. He has always kept his prices down so that he is affordable to those in need of his services. Indeed, he did not raise his price for fifteen years, and then only did so when a client who had been to him for years recommended that he should. He has never exploited anyone in any way using his ability.

Kevin described himself as "...the total opposite of a narcissist...two of the things I hate are narcissism and hypocrisy," both of which he has witnessed in the medium world.

"I like to be anonymous. I love doing my thing and then going out having a cup of coffee."

To him, mediumship is just a part of his life, "It's just a natural thing that's happened since I've been a little kid. I don't make much of it."

He doesn't advertise himself as a medium while working at his full-time job as a flight attendant. In fact, he has done little advertising over the last twenty-five years, with his web presence basically kept up by the radio/TV sponsors or the psychic's office staff. He initially relied mainly on word of mouth for decades and his reputation kept his schedule as busy as he could handle for the most part.

Witness to the World Beyond   83

In the early years, when asked by colleagues at the airline if he had a second job, he simply said, "Yes, real estate." That is, he recalled with a smile, until a pilot called him once at home asking for his realtor expertise to help finding a new home. From that moment on, he was honest when asked, come what may with the varied reactions. At this point, many of his colleagues know of his ability and have been read by him so it is no longer something that he hides, but he still doesn't bring it up in conversations.

Among those who were interviewed for this book, there were many common attributes to describe Kevin: caring, selfless, conscientious, empathetic, shy, reclusive, smart, well-read, honest, humble, modest, funny, kind, soft-spoken, genuine, down to earth, authentic, extremely talented, exceptional, very concrete, specific, no nonsense, and "right on the money." His accuracy was described as "dead on" (pun intended by the interviewee). Those who knew him well commented that he maintains a low profile and overall is a "wonderful, wonderful man."

Candice described him as a "very blunt man who doesn't project himself as a medium. You would never know if you met him or bumped into him in the store. He is who he is and he doesn't let anything else influence that."

Similarly, when asked to describe Kevin, Paul M. jokingly replied, "An Irish accountant! That hasn't done my taxes!"

Kevin simply was not what he expected the first time he went to a medium party at a friend's home. Over several decades he has come to know Kevin as a friend and described him further as: "friendly, jovial, kind, caring and considerate."

Nancy, who considers Kevin a friend as well as a medium, commented, "I think he is so understated. I don't know how to describe it but I think the fact that he's just so human, and he looks just like us, is the reason I felt so comfortable. I think if he had like a crystal ball, or something I would have turned around!" [laughs].

Wendy Smith gave a description of Kevin, "Amazing, selfless, very selfless. He's very caring and conscientious, very kind, soft-spoken. He is absolutely the real deal."

Elaine Simmons explained her view of Kevin as a professional vs. Kevin as a friend:

> "He's almost like an actor when he does his readings. During the readings, he's very professional…he's serious, involved and he's paying attention. After he's done with his job, he comes out and he's like the life of the party. He's really funny. He's a really kind, kind soul. He's thoughtful, he's sweet. And he's a really good friend. He would do anything for you, anything."

Liv Ullmann, the esteemed actress and director, periodically connects with Kevin for readings. She commented that, "He is not a loner, he sees people and has friends, but…it's a lonely gift to have."

Similarly, Candice reflected that, "It's probably a very lonely feeling for him because like…is this person really my friend? Or is this person just trying to pump me for info, right?"

Wendy Golini spoke of him as a cherished friend and Kevin is considered an honorary beloved uncle to her children. She shared:

"He is one of the dearest people to me. He is very modest with his gifts; he won't exploit them. When you see Kevin coming in, he's not what you would envision [for someone] that has embraced the spirit world. Kevin does not; he looks like he stepped out of a J. Crew catalog, very preppy, very quiet, very well read. But when he gives his gift to others, the affirmation is priceless to people, priceless."

And yet, Wendy G. later noted that his self-esteem on occasion needs boosting from his friends as a result of his upbringing by "tough Irish parents."

Those who know him well also commented that he is very professional, "black and white", "no nonsense" and gets down to business quickly during a reading but he is a very different and funny guy when he is relaxing with friends. Marie, who has become Kevin's friend over the years, commented, as did several others, that "he is a lot of fun and funny" as well as "very intuitive."

Among those that knew Kevin personally, all agreed that he was not looking for the limelight.

As Deborah Coull shared, "If he were another person and not shy, he could be in another whole realm of success…and you know, showcased. But he just doesn't have it in him."

Liz Baker concurred with this, "He is amazingly shy and reclusive. He doesn't like a lot of fuss. He prefers to be in the background. He doesn't like being the star of the show at all."

Alan initially met Kevin at a medium house party but now after approximately fifteen years, he considers him a friend "who is fun to hang around with. And he's busy, he's definitively busy."

Alan also noted that, "He is funny, dry humor, you know? Kevin doesn't take anyone's BS and likes to avoid drama at all costs."

Kevin thought long and hard about having a book written about himself. He is not seeking fame and gets nervous generally when speaking in front of others, although he "hides" this fear well when doing medium readings in large groups. So, what was his purpose for collaborating on this project?

"People love the stories… my job is to prove the continuity of life."

He wanted to share his life story and "what is normal for me and for what I know. And maybe possibly to enlighten someone. But I'm not trying to convert anybody. If you don't want to believe, that's your business."

At the end of the day, Kevin considers himself an average guy with an uncommon ability who has been told countless times that he has changed people's lives in a positive way through his readings.

"Like I said, I just love a normal life. I don't need fame. I don't need people to tell me how wonderful I am. Being a medium isn't who I am, it's what I do."

Part III: Evidence From the "Real McCoy"

"My job as a medium is to prove the continuity of life, it's not to tell you how to hit the jackpot number."

Kevin Coan (2020)

"At the end of the day, I've got people that have faith in me. I don't care what the rest of the world thinks."

Kevin Coan (2020)

Chapter 9: "Frozen in Grief," Learning to Live Again After the Loss of a Child

Joe Leblanc and his wife of forty-three years, Marilyn, were briefly introduced in Chapter 7. They sought Kevin's medium services after they had lost their son Joey, the only child that they had together. He died in a small airplane crash while on what was meant to be a fun, late evening cruise in the skies with a friend over twenty years ago, at age twenty-nine.

Marilyn had come into the marriage with three other children as well. It was Joe's first marriage. Joe had grown up very poor, one of three sons in a two-bedroom home with no central heating until they were well into their teens. He started working for cash when he was eleven. He became a brick layer by trade but also was a successful business man eventually, owning multiple rental properties and a bar. He had just finished building Joey a new home in their same town three months prior to his death.

Joe and his wife were overwhelmed with grief after Joey's sudden death. Joe couldn't sleep and wouldn't go upstairs to bed. He would stay up on the couch all night and hold his son's watch in his hands for comfort. Joe and Marilyn both went to Kevin for years and received confirmation that their child's spirit was there. Joe shared in the interview:

> "It's amazing what he [Kevin] came in with. He'd bring us comfort just to show that the spirits are still around you. He proves the continuity of life after death. He tells you things that nobody else knows. And that's the best way to explain it. He's the real McCoy."

On the first visit, Kevin said to Joe, "Joey told me to tell you, you don't have to hold his watch in your hand any more. He's there with you."

Marilyn looked at her husband and asked, "You hold the watch in your hand?"

"Yeah," Joe replied.

"She never knew it; nobody knew it," Joe explained in the interview.

For years after their son's death, they continued to see Kevin regularly to connect with their son. Meanwhile, early on they found themselves in a new legal battle soon after the death of their son once the official autopsy came in. They had already buried the remains they were given of their son after his Catholic funeral Mass, with over six hundred people in attendance. The final autopsy report came several weeks after the services. Joe noticed it mentioned that their son was a circumcised male. Alas, he realized, they had been given the remains of his friend, the pilot, as Joey was not circumcised. Both had been burned beyond recognition in the fiery crash so they had not originally looked into the delivered bags of his now buried remains.

It took "eight years, four or five lawyers, and approximately $120,000" to get it straightened out. They did not care about or need the settlement money but wanted to improve regulations related to small plane pilot qualifications. During this stressful period, they were able to find some solace through Kevin's readings; they met with him every five or six months. Kevin became a lifelong friend and part of the family.

Joe would experience yet another horrible tragedy ten years after Joey's death. His beloved wife Marilyn would get metastatic colon cancer. As she lay critically ill in the hospital room one day, Joe left the room briefly and met with Kevin in the hospital lobby. He had come to visit them. Joe discussed her grave condition. Kevin told Joe to go back to her room as Marilyn was going to "see their son Joey."

As soon as Joe returned to the room, Marilyn greeted him with, "There's Joey standing in the doorway. He's standing right there in the doorway."

Joe could not see him but replied, "Oh yeah."

Joe choked up with emotion during the interview as he shared his last words with his wife several days after she saw the apparition of their son. He sat holding her hand before she passed and said to her, "Go to Joey." It was a small comfort to know that she had seen their son and that she believed that Joey would be there to greet her as she passed. Marilyn died in November of 2011. As a close friend now, Kevin typically visits and calls Joe regularly. He also gives him a reading every Christmas to help minimize Joe's loneliness over the holiday.

In the few weeks before the interview for this book in 2021, Joe would face loss once again. His best friend who had lived for thirty years in an apartment that Joe had built for him over his own garage had died from cancer at age sixty-eight the week prior. He had also lost a faithful companion, his dog Angel, one month ago.

"My dog really, really took a toll on me because we were close for the last part of my life, you know? You have to live with it, the pain. You don't like it, but you live with the pain."

Joe never went regularly to grief counseling after the death of his son or wife; he tried it one time but found it "very cliquey." He found solace instead through Kevin's readings that connected him to his loved ones.

In addition to communication through Kevin from his son and wife, Joe has also received hundreds of messages over the past twenty years from many others through Kevin, including his parents, a brother, in-laws and friends who have passed. And Kevin has always been "right on the money."

Joe's father died at age fifty-three and it was Joe who would take over the responsibility to care for his mother out of the three sons.

Kevin shared words from his father, "You were always the best one of the bunch. Out of the three, I knew you would take care of your mother."

Joe found that "very, very comforting" to hear.

His mother sent a similar message, "I don't worry much about you because I know you can take care of yourself."

She worried more about the other two brothers who both had run into tough times during their lives. His parents also passed on that he and his wife Marilyn had done a "wonderful job" raising their son Joey. Marilyn's stepmother Barb and her husband John also came through to thank Joe for buying John an accessible vehicle and building a ramp for him when he became disabled and required a wheelchair due to neuropathy.

In one reading Kevin told him, "I got John here and he appreciates all the thoughtfulness, it didn't go unnoticed."

At eighty-three, Joe has suffered enormous sorrows. He has had his share of health challenges as well.

At one informal house reading, Kevin told Joe, "You were standing at your kitchen sink last night and you said out loud, I can't die tonight. I'm Frank Sinatra."

Joe asked, "Was Joey [his son] there?"

Kevin smiled and said, "Well, I wasn't there so it would have had to have been him."

Joe had exclaimed those exact words as he was taking his prescribed pills the night before. He was borrowing from Sinatra's famous quote, "I'm gonna live 'til I die."

Despite his share of health ailments, Joe remains quite active and full of life, having recently purchased a new puppy, Angel Two. The main consolation that Joe kept repeating in his interview was the realization through Kevin's readings that he was never truly alone. Indeed, during one reading, Kevin told him that Marilyn said that he [Joe] had been saying "he's all alone."

Her message was, "You're never alone. We're always with you."

A lifelong practicing Catholic, Joe noted, "They tell you there's life after death. But they don't show no proof. I always believed in life after death but I wasn't guaranteed on it 'til he [Kevin] brought everything in with the reads."

Kevin has provided evidence to Joe, many times over, that there is a form of life after death. This has been a great consolation during his time of sorrow.

Sheila Cedrone is a married, retired school teacher. She first had a reading with Kevin after her father died in 1996. She recalled that it was a really good experience at the time. Kevin would relay a conversation that she had recently or identify a certain song that she had listened to when her dad was there. She went a few times again over the next seven years until she and her husband tragically lost their only son, Jared, in 2003. He was twenty-three years old and died from complications of a car accident. Her son also suffered from drug addiction.

"After Jared first passed, I was desperate to make a connection. I had gone to the Spiritualist church a few times."

She ended up signing up for an unfoldment class when Kevin was teaching them. Kevin would bring Jared through almost weekly. She realized that she had a little bit of intuitiveness but was not going to be a medium herself. Still, it was comforting, albeit bittersweet, to have her son come through often via Kevin. She explained:

> "When I first went to him after Jared passed, he described that Jared was in an auto accident and that he was drug addicted. What amazed me at the time was that he described the scene at the hospital. He had been at the hospital for about a month. The day he was passing, he described the scene and what was going on in the hospital room. It was pretty amazing."

Witness to the World Beyond   95

Another interesting reading involving Jared revolved around a turquoise outfit that she had bought. Shelia mentioned that she generally doesn't wear a lot of colorful clothes. When she tried the new outfit on for her husband he responded, "Yeah, too blue."

At the next reading, Kevin told her that her son wanted to tell her, "You should have kept the blue outfit, it looked great."

Sheila described a deceased cousin of hers who had been "a character" in life. He had happened to die while still in a lot of debt. Her husband jokingly ran around the house singing, "I'm debt free! I'm debt free!" mimicking the cousin's freedom from debt after his death. Her deceased son Jared showed Kevin that scene and at the next reading Kevin clearly described her husband's joking behavior to Sheila.

Sheila lost her mother in 2010, seven years after Jared's death. While she was in hospice Sheila would say to her, "When you get there, will you please take care of my Jared?"

After her mother died, at the next reading she had with Kevin, he told her that her mother's message was, "I'm not taking care of Jared. He is taking care of me."

After her mother's death, Sheila's sister worried about what to do with all their mother's beautiful things. Her mother also came through with the message to her sister, "Things are not important, so don't worry about them."

Kevin recalled one of his memorable stories about a reading that he gave to a woman who had recently lost her daughter in a car accident. At one point Kevin told her, "I want you to know that I see a picture frame with the words

"Twinkle Twinkle Little Star" written on the edge of the frame. Your daughter made that happen."

"Oh my God! A few months ago, I was shopping in a Pier 1 Imports store and saw a picture frame with those words on it. I desperately wanted to buy it but needed to pick up a present for someone and didn't bring my credit card," the woman responded.

She didn't think to tell the clerk to hold it for her. Instead, she foolishly hid the frame on a remote shelf in the store. When she returned it was gone and the clerks had no idea what it was and couldn't find it in the inventory to order it again for her.

"My daughter's up there with the stars," she used to tell her other living daughter all the time and thus the frame would have been perfect.

Within a week after being unable to purchase it at the store, she had received a box of Christmas gifts from her deceased daughter's friends. At the bottom of the box was the very same frame with the "Twinkle, Twinkle Little Star" inscription with a picture of her daughter in it. Without knowing any of this, Kevin was able to provide comfort to this woman by telling her that her daughter had made that happen.

Another story recalled by Kevin involved a reading after the death by suicide of a woman's son. Kevin read her at a home in the North Shore region of Massachusetts. Her son came through right away. Kevin told the woman that he knew her son had hung himself in the garage.

"Yes," she replied.

She explained to Kevin that his death was totally unexpected. He had been an excellent student but had been bullied and harassed at school.

"Your son knows about the rabbits at the cemetery and it's definitely ok with him," Kevin told her at one point.

"Oh my God! I tend to my son's grave all the time. I put flowers there and the rabbits keep eating the flowers. A woman that tends her husband's grave nearby told me a week ago that she feels really bad that the rabbits seem to be only eating the flowers at my son's grave but nobody else's."

She had replied to the woman at the cemetery, "Something tells me that my son would think it was okay."

And those were the exact words that Kevin heard her son tell him from beyond. It brought a bit of comfort to the woman during her time of unimaginable grief.

Kevin also recalled a father coming to him for a reading after his son Chris had committed suicide.

What Kevin remembered telling him at one point was, "You have an orange tabby cat."

"Yes, I do," the man acknowledged.

"Just yesterday you were reading the paper on the couch and the cat was staring at the wall and then turning its head and staring at you. It did this repeatedly. You got up from the couch and said to the wall *Is that you Chris?*"

"I was! I just did that last night!" the man replied in shock.

Kevin explained to the father that he could see that because his son Chris showed the scene to him. It was a bit of evidence that his spirit was still somewhere and had been with his father the evening before. Again, the gift was a welcome comfort for this grieving parent.

At a group reading in his friend Darlyne's office, Kevin brought a woman to tears one day. But they were tears of gratitude. As he looked at the picture one woman brought, he was able to bring through her mother and give some evidence from the beyond that was specific to her.

Kevin told her, "You have others close to you that have passed, including a son."

"Yes! Turn over my mother's picture," responded the woman.

He did so and saw a picture of a little baby boy.

Kevin said, "This baby was smothered with a pillow while you were out getting milk."

The woman screamed. Kevin continued, "Yes, and your husband murdered your son."

With a ragged voice while hyperventilating, the woman responded:

> "I went out to buy milk and I came back and my son had died. Many years later, when my then ex-husband was dying of cancer, he called me and had a death bed confession. He said he had killed our son."

"I just want you to know you are always sitting on the edge of your bed asking your mother to watch over your son, which she obviously is. You are also always asking for her forgiveness. She wants you to know, you are her daughter and there is nothing to forgive," Kevin replied.

Later that evening the woman spoke to Kevin privately and said, "I've been in therapy for thirty-something years. I now feel like I could cancel my next appointment after your reading."

Nancy is a retired school teacher who currently works part-time as an educator. Nancy and her husband had two children, a son and a daughter, until the unimaginable happened to their family. The youngest, their daughter Amelia, called from her college dorm in Boston one Tuesday out of the blue and asked if her mother and father wanted to take her out to dinner in Boston that night. The parents were both working at the time of the call – one in a suburb west of Boston and the other in the South Shore area so they would have to leave from work separately to meet up with her in the city.

It was a spur of the moment request, but she had a paper to write later that evening and Amelia just wanted to see them and have a good meal before she focused on the work ahead of her. They decided to come in despite the unplanned inconvenience and took her out to dinner in Boston, not far from her dorm. She was a freshman and had already made friends at school and was quite a happy, well-adjusted and loving child. Amelia was also a loyal, funny and smart young woman. She was loved by all, including animals and people. She was multi-talented as well, as an artist, writer and amazing mimic.

Since her early days as a young child, Amelia was afraid of the dark and remained so as she entered college. Amelia was a well-adjusted, responsible, cautious and remarkable young woman. Their last view of her alive was of her walking back to her dorm after their dinner together.

Later that night, around 1:00 am, Amelia and a friend from school decided to go out for a walk. Behind the dorm was a well-used path that led to a train track where students often would hang out. Being from the suburbs, Nancy used to warn Amelia about the dangers of the trolley trains along the main street of the university but she hadn't realized that there was a high-speed train only a short walk behind their dorms. There was a common path to these train tracks with a broken fence that had been beaten down for some time.

The Emergency Medical Technicians (EMTs) who had responded to the scene of the accident later told Nancy and her husband that the two students hadn't walked very far down the track – they had turned around to go back from where they entered the track when they were hit from behind. The engine was at the back of a seven-car train and there were snowbanks along the tracks. Both of these conditions would have reduced the noise of the oncoming train. The train engineer saw the two students when they were only fifty feet in front of the train. He didn't have time to blow a horn, flash emergency lights or come to a stop in time. Both of the students died instantly.

The morning after their last dinner together, Nancy heard about a fatal accident involving two university students during her commute to work and felt uneasy, but not alarmed. It couldn't be her daughter, she told herself. Later that day police came and cordoned off the public school where Nancy was working. She was questioned by the MBTA transit police as they tried to figure out if there were any underlying causes for the accident. All toxicology tests were later negative, as expected by Nancy and her husband. She recalled sadly:

> "I just remember thinking this isn't true, it didn't happen, you're lying. And getting very angry, it seemed so preposterous because I kept saying I don't know what you're talking about…the trolleys wouldn't be running at two o'clock in the morning. I

couldn't picture where on campus this happened. It was really pretty horrific."

Nancy asked the school to at least fix the broken fence immediately; it took seven months but they eventually repaired the fence. It took many years later for some of the Trustees to meet with them; one of them finally apologized.

During the initial period of shock and grief, Nancy threw herself into a whirlwind of activity such as scholarship drives in her daughter's name and planning one fundraiser after another to support the scholarships.

But when asked how she was during this frenzy, she recalls responding, "I'm frozen; my husband is frozen."

To everyone she ran into including friends, family, doctors, colleagues, religious leaders, psychological counselors, and members of a Compassionate Friends group, she'd ask: "Where is she? Is she safe? Is she warm? She is really afraid of the dark…"

No one could answer her questions.

"They'd look at me and think 'I don't know.' They didn't know how to respond to me."

She did get some comfort from a rabbi who honestly responded, "I don't know if bad things happen, but I'm going to say it's a better place. I'm shocked that all this stuff happens. I can't answer it. I don't know what to tell you."

Approximately a year after the death of her daughter Amelia, the President of the Compassionate Friends group took Nancy aside at one point and said, "Nancy, you keep asking the same questions at these meetings. We can't answer them but there's somebody out there that can answer those questions possibly."

She gave her two names and contact numbers. One was a Catholic nun living in Philadelphia who gave helpful grief counseling over the phone. But she couldn't allay all her fears and answer her worrisome questions. Nancy and her husband weren't familiar with the medium world and so she called her close friend Jane for advice about the second name given to her, Kevin V. Coan.

Jane's response was, "All they're going to do is google you. They're going to say something awful. They could be creepy, like talk as if they are Amelia."

Jane was concerned for her friend Nancy and her husband; it could be a devastating experience as they were still raw with shock and grief. Desperate for someone to answer her questions, Nancy was willing to take the risk.

Her friend Jane said, "Okay. I'll call, I'll make the appointment. You just use my check. I don't want him knowing anything about you."

When Nancy and her husband arrived at the Wellness Center in a gym type building, they first saw a "...guy with a Red Sox baseball cap on. He looked like a regular person."

He looked at them and asked, "Ahh, you're here for the medium?"

When they responded yes, he advised them to wait in the waiting room.

Then at the time of the appointment he came back and said, "Follow me."

"Oh, are you the medium?" Nancy asked once they sat in a private room.

He smiled and shook his head yes and said, "You might want to turn on your tape recorder."

They were put at ease with him immediately despite noticing right away his rather odd way of appearing to be

Witness to the World Beyond   103

talking to someone who is not visible in the room and hesitating at times as if he is listening to someone.

Soon he said, "I'm in this car, it's been in an accident. I see a lot of smoke and flames…. this is horrible."

Nancy and her husband were mute and in shock; this didn't sound like Amelia's accident.

But then immediately Kevin said, "Wait a minute, change the channel, there's something wrong here. I'm getting a cross wire. Give me a minute to regroup."

Later Nancy would realize that he was seeing the fatal accident of the nephew of her friend Jane but at the time, she and her husband were confused.

Soon, Kevin resumed, "Ok, let me start again. I am at an ATM and there's something written under where you put the card in. It looks like I'm in …." [identifies the section of Boston where she attended school].

He then mentioned, "Tacos are always great, even though some people are vegetarians."

Nancy recognized right away the ATM near the taco place where Amelia frequented (which she noted during the interview had graffiti written underneath the card placement slot when she later checked it out). Kevin kept jumping from one scene to another.

"I'm seeing a water tower now, so I'm someplace else. And there's a girl with really wild curly hair…I think your daughter or somebody's telling me about the poet."

Amelia's best friend had rather untamed curly hair and Amelia's nickname for her was "the poet."

He continued, "I'm sort of someplace like maybe [mentions a town on the South Shore]? I'm on a beach, but it's not X Beach." [names a local beach in that town].

Nancy and her husband said the town he mentioned sounded right. They had not told him that they lived there.

Nancy suggested, "Y Beach?" [other beach in town where Amelia and her friends liked to hang out].

"Yeah…and I see a lot of friends and I see her there."

And then he switched gears once again and said, "And now I see a really awful accident. I used to work for Amtrak. Did you know that?"

They responded, "No."

Kevin continued, "Yeah sometimes people are near the tracks and we can't stop… you know someone is telling me that you're in your car that morning and you hear some news about some kids that got hit by a train. You feel very uneasy and then in … [names town where she worked that day] later all this stuff is happening.…. but your mother was with you. Didn't you smell the lily of the valley?"

Nancy recalled that she was just so stunned, shocked and frozen by this time, all she could manage was to nod her head yes on occasion during the reading.

Kevin went on jumping from Amelia's friends' descriptions, to Nancy and her husband's house, Amelia's room and identified the specific pattern of their dinner plates. As he described them eating off the plates recently, he said he wanted Nancy to know that her mother or her daughter were there and that is how he could describe the scenes, - from them. He also gave detailed descriptions of her living son which were amazingly on target.

At one point Kevin mentioned, "You really ought to open the closet and look in that box of hers. There's going to be something in that box from her that's going to make a difference to you."

Nancy later found a notebook of Amelia's in a box at the bottom of the closet. In it were various calligraphy-inspired doodles of hers which they later took pictures of and made into stationery that they sold for the scholarship

Witness to the World Beyond   105

fund. But also, more importantly, there was a one-page essay written by Amelia, date unknown. It was about an Old Testament story found in the Book of Job which spoke of joy and suffering. It was beautifully written and almost served as a premonition of the suffering that they were enduring after her tragic death and the reminder to appreciate the joy in life. Nancy checked with Amelia's college professors and none said it was for their course; she wasn't taking courses in philosophy or religion at the time.

"She just talked about how there's joy in the world, that things can be hard but you have to be hopeful. I mean I felt it was speaking to me."

Kevin assured Nancy and her husband during that first session that Amelia was "a good kid…it had nothing to do with that…" [meaning she was not responsible for the accident in any way].

"She was in the wrong place, but it was her time."

When Nancy asked her own questions about safety and warmth and the dark, finally he was the one person who could respond with a kind smile, "I can answer that question."

He described her being with all sorts of animals, helping them cross over.

"And she's going to work with kids because she really feels she can do more, from where she is now to help others and her friends. She's still watching out for you. And yes, she's okay."

He also told her to pay more attention to signs from Amelia.

"When you look up into the night light, haven't you seen a plane go right up overhead or a star suddenly look likes it's twinkling or a cardinal in a weird season? Those are all your daughter. Those are signs she's sending you."

Toward the end of one of many sessions, Kevin told them, "She said before you leave, she has one message for you: She's really busy, you've got to get it together. You know, it's okay, you've got to live your life. Stop asking about what would Amelia do? It's more important to ask–what are you going to do about it?"

Nancy replied, "Yeah, you're right, I just want to be the best parent I could be in the whole world. I want to make her proud of me."

"Well then go do it!" Kevin responded.

Nancy laughed during the interview as she recalled this recommendation from her daughter. She remembers thinking and feeling so much more hopeful since that moment. She shared a written tribute of her daughter with me after the interview:

> "My daughter Amelia was a lively, loyal person that was a natural mimic. She could impersonate teachers, her principal, and members of our family with an incredible accuracy! Everyone ended up laughing, even those she imitated. She loved all animals and they often followed her home from the middle school. She warmly greeted the cats, dogs, and squirrels in our neighborhood and even named many of the crows in our yard at a young age. One of her cats, Hercules, had been rescued from a local dumpster and she found him at the animal shelter. Amelia nursed Hercules back to health by feeding him medicine every three hours and he lived many wonderful years with her.
>
> Amelia had so many dreams for her future including becoming an architect to design a building that would welcome and support families and their pets. She was creative and made many colorful

unique purses, messenger bags, belts, and shoes out of duct tape. All of her jobs, endeavors, and interests improved the lives of her friends, family, animals, particularly felines, and those around her. She loved to journal, write poetry, create elaborate doodles, and make interesting art work that often had many textural features.

Amelia was a curious but cautious child who always slept with a night light and did not get her license as a teenager after a classmate was killed in a drunken driving accident. She became the designated "passenger" however and mother hen of her group of friends and was often the voice of reason. I later found a bucket list of things she wanted to accomplish before she was thirty years old including driving to California with friends in a VW bus, falling in love, having children, and building a special wing on the animal shelter for older dogs and cats with many toys and free massages.

Amelia had so much to live for and loved going to college and meeting new people. Her death shocked our family, her friends, and members of our town. No one could believe that this had happened to her. My family was supported by the outpouring of love from so many people, many of whom we had never even met but who knew Amelia or were touched by her story. My focus became to honor her life and legacy and become the best parent I could be in her memory. I try to focus now on the present and all the wonderful things happening around us instead of worrying and planning so much in the future. She was an incredibly magical person that really relished every minute of her life. There is so much I don't know about life or why things happen, but I do know our love for Amelia lives on and her love for us supports us every day."

After that first reading by Kevin, Nancy recalled, "Oh I don't know what he did, but it was a miracle. I think I drove home and my husband was like…stunned."

She has seen him three more times over the years, once in a group restaurant open reading with her friend Jane, who is now a believer in his ability. Despite her ongoing grief for the loss of her child, Nancy has experienced profound gratitude for having Amelia in her life, albeit too briefly. Amelia has impacted all of her family's lives and changed them in a way that helps them as they move forward day after day by honoring her memory in countless ways.

At one reading Kevin told her and her husband, "Amelia was with you when you were looking at turtles."

Nancy laughed and said to her husband, "Please give Kevin his present now." It was a box of chocolate covered turtles.

Over the years Kevin has given Nancy some advice on her work, insights about her living son's life and his work and all were "on target" even if some of them came to fruition months later. She concluded:

"I think people want to know, at least I did, that she was someplace and she was still existing in some form, some place. I really do think he's incredibly gifted and kind. He can give something to someone in a way that's so factual and realistic, that really lifts and boosts them out of where they are. It was just a miracle, it is something that we couldn't do ourselves, we couldn't get through therapy or from other parents. He gave us a purpose. We wanted to know if she still was someplace. And he could answer that question. He saved our lives in a lot of ways; I really do believe he did."

Chapter 10: The Continuity of Life – A Bit of Comfort and Peace

Brian Phillips, a retired legal compliance officer for a nationally known insurance company, was aware of Kevin's abilities through his spouse and a close friend but was never interested in having a reading himself. After his own mother died, Brian still waited a year to see a medium as the grief was "too raw" to contemplate going before that. He went with his sister for a joint reading with Kevin V. Coan, she the skeptic, and he the believer in mediumship. Brian's first impression of Kevin was that "he was very personable, easy to talk to and just very down to earth." Kevin was dressed informally, wearing a sweatshirt, which made Brian and his sister feel relaxed and comfortable in the small office where they met with him.

Brian's mother Pat had a hard life but she never complained and always counted her blessings. Her husband had left her to raise their four children when Brian, the eldest, was in his early teens. They moved in with her grandparents and parents on a farm in Massachusetts. Pat went to work at AT&T to provide for her family and never missed a day's work. As the oldest son, Brian felt guilty that he couldn't do more to ease her burden during his upbringing, although he was always a dutiful and loving son and remained so until her final days. Pat suffered through several bouts of different cancers in her last decade and had deteriorated significantly during the last few years of her life.

The picture Brian had brought to his reading with Kevin was of his mother's last birthday celebration with his siblings. Kevin knew right away that Pat had passed and told them that she was communicating with him. He relayed that she was "no longer suffering, she wasn't in pain." That reassurance was comforting to them, but still, as Brian noted, "anybody could have told us that of course." But then Kevin's reading got more specific.

"You saw a suncatcher today, didn't you, when you were walking?"

"Yes, I actually did. I was walking by somebody's garden and I saw the suncatcher."

"Well, your mom was there."

Kevin explained that she had been with him and saw that. "She wanted to pass that along by way of me to reassure you that I was connected with her."

And then Kevin continued, "So, you had a cat cut across your path the other day and that's unusual?"

"Well, yeah, I live in a city and there are not a lot of stray cats in my neighborhood. But in fact, a couple of days ago when I was walking down my street, a cat walked in front of me."

"Well, your mom was there too. She saw that."

Kevin also commented to Brian that his father had not been a support for the family. His mother had to be resilient because she could not rely on him.

"Your mother was a very, very hard-working woman, wasn't she?"

"Yeah."

"Well, she never regretted that. She wants you to know that she had a very good life. She had no regrets."

Brian had also been routinely visiting his mother's gravesite to tend it, despite the two-hour round-way trip. He would leave fresh flowers, play a Patsy Cline song for her and leave a card at her headstone. Kevin let Brian know that his mother was aware of him at the cemetery plot but told him he "didn't have to feel compelled to be doing that." She was still with him, on some level, wherever he was. That was a comfort and took the pressure off of him. Henceforth, Brian celebrated her in the same small ways but from his own home.

Brian noted, "But beyond that, it was a reassurance that he gave me about her current state. He didn't go into a lot of details about where she was but I wasn't as concerned about that. It's just knowing she is past suffering."

Kevin then asked Brian at one point during the reading, "Who's Barbara?"

"My grandmother's name was Barbara."

"She's here. She wanted to let you know she has your back; she's looking out for you."

Alison Blake is a part-time fitness trainer in her fifties. She is married and the mother of three children. She grew up in the same town as Kevin and was his sister Kathy's close friend since childhood. She remembered Kevin being quiet as a child, "a little serious and a little introverted." But with the three-year age difference, they really did not cross paths much.

Describing Kevin today, Alison explained, "He's still very quiet, kind of mysterious. I'm fascinated by him, though. He's the real deal for sure."

Alison has had two readings by Kevin. She mentioned a couple of things from these readings that really stood out. Her father and father-in-law had died less than a year apart. At one reading with her husband, as noted in Chapter 7, Kevin immediately knew his father was a cigar smoker. And he saw him with his friend who had died after a fall from the roof of a church.

The second most memorable reading was when Alison took her mother to see Kevin after her father had passed. Alison first explained the background of the story. After her father died, her mother had to move into low-income housing to a very small room. She and her sister had just helped her move and they were trying to fit some of her old furniture in the new space with little luck. In the kitchenette, they didn't have room for her old table.

She and her sister said to her, "Mom, you need a table. We'll have to look for a tiny table."

"No, no, I can just eat my meals sitting in the sofa with the coffee table."

The three of them talked back and forth about a new small table.

At the next reading, Kevin said to her mother, "Your husband says you should buy the table."

Alison recalled, "There was no question about what he was talking about."

Kevin also told their mother when she had come for a reading, "When you are looking out your window, doing the dishes and you hear the train go by, your husband is with you."

Again, they knew exactly what he was talking about as her new kitchen window looked out onto a train track.

Alison's one brother was particularly close to her father. She explained, "they played cribbage all the time, that was their bonding thing."

Kevin saw and reported that as well. He told Alison and her mother, "I can see your father liked to play cards. I'm not sure what card game it is, if it's poker or cribbage or another card game but he liked to play with your son. Your husband spends a lot of time with your son on Route 62."

Indeed, Alison's brother had recently moved to an apartment on Route 62 in Danvers, MA.

While many of these communications brought peace and comfort to Alison and her family members, some of the readings included less serious but equally evidential tidbits from her passed loved ones.

For example, at one reading Kevin told Alison, "You have a large door in your house that is broken. A large door."

"No, I don't."

"Yes, you do, you do."

"No!" Alison responded.

"I'm not backing away from it and it is a big door."

An hour later, it dawned on Alison, "Oh my God, my garage door doesn't work!"

Kevin wasn't going to back down even when she denied it.

At another reading Kevin asked, "Do you have a shell collection in your house?"

"No, I don't collect shells."

"Do you have shells in your house?"

Witness to the World Beyond   115

"No."

"Now I am seeing that you have a shell collection – it is being moved around from room to room."

"I promise you I do not have a shell collection in my house. I especially don't have anything that travels from room to room."

"Ok, I'm not backing away from it, there's a shell collection here," Kevin responded once again.

Only later, hours after the reading, did Alison recall that when her daughter was a toddler, she loved to play with two conch shells. She'd hold them and walk around the house with them.

Kevin later explained to her that he had seen it as a silent picture. He can see it but he doesn't know how it makes sense.

"So, he's telling me what he's seeing. We have to put it together."

Alison admitted that she was not a believer in mediums until she had readings with Kevin.

Patricia is a retired nurse in her sixties. She was generally too busy earlier in her life to consider going to a psychic or medium, both of whom she thought "just made-up stuff" for the most part. She had gone to one psychic that was pretty right on when her father was ill however. When she heard of Kevin's reputation and that he did readings in the same office as that psychic, she booked an appointment. She had lost both her father and brother at that point.

Patricia described her first and only appointment with Kevin to date, "So right away he asked me about my father, where he lived and worked. He noted that this man had problems with his chest or throat area."

Her father had suffered a heart attack and stroke before his death and was left unable to speak. Kevin noted that both her father and brother worked for utilities or the phone company. Her brother had been an electrician and her father worked as a lineman who climbed telephone poles. Kevin also said that he was getting a feeling of concern associated with someone who has severe memory issues but it is not Alzheimer's disease. Patricia replied that could be her mother who was currently having memory issues or her sister who is alive with severe brain damage.

"Who's the one with cancer that really spread? He went down very quickly and people were surprised."

"That was my brother who died four weeks after his cancer diagnosis."

Kevin was able to bring much comfort to Patricia through messages from her father and her brother.

Over and over again he said, "Your father just wants the best for you…your father is really proud of you…. all he wants is for you to be happy."

These were more general messages that of course could have been told to her by anyone. However, he also shared with her many, very specific details of her family's life and messages that no one could have known.

"Was your father deaf in one ear?" Kevin then mimicked someone cupping a hand to one ear and said, "He's going like this."

Patricia confirmed that her father was deaf in one ear early in his life and later became deaf in both ears.

"Well, he can hear now," Kevin said with a smile.

Patricia recalled that at the time, "I just loved that. I was so excited because he could finally hear just fine."

Patricia did not share with Kevin that she had a recent divorce but he was aware of it nonetheless. Her father sent the message that he was never really crazy about her former husband, although he wouldn't have ever told her that. He gave her permission, without judgment, to have followed through with this painful decision; he gave his approval. Another little bit of comfort that made her smile.

Kevin also picked up on alcohol issues in her former husband's family as well as among a close friend of Patricia's. Kevin was nonjudgmental when identifying this issue and even shared that he understands about this as both of his parents were alcoholics. He asked if a close friend of hers had back or neck problems.

"Not that I know of," she replied.

"Well keep that in mind," Kevin responded.

The next morning, her friend called to say, "I woke up with the worst stiff neck, what can I do for this pain?"

As mentioned in Chapter 7, Kevin also described the personalities and characteristics of Patricia's two grown children and four grandchildren with specifics that were unique to each.

Patricia summarized her impression of her reading as one that "made me firmer in my belief in the afterlife and …just very comforted by the feeling that he's there [her father], he's watching and seeing what's going on."

Liv Ullmann, the internationally acclaimed Norwegian actor, director, author and humanitarian, met Kevin V. Coan through a mutual friend in the US. Although she has had approximately seven readings with him over the past decade, there was one "incredible" story she recalled from her first reading that she is eternally grateful for. First, she explained the backstory:

"He asked me to bring a picture and I brought the picture of my daughter Linn's father. He was twenty-one years older than me and he had been dead for many years, actually ten or some years when I met Kevin. He and I always said to each other, 'When one of us dies, we have to come back and show ourselves to the other one.' I wasn't living with him because by then I had married Donald. But we were the truest, truest of friends and we worked together. 'Don't come back as a fly or something because what if you harm the fly?' - we had all these funny things we promised each other. And then I was there on the last evening and night of his life. I went to Sweden. He was Swedish. And maybe he didn't know I was there because he was on his way. I said, 'I'm here. I think you called me.' I said these things but I don't know if he ever heard it. And then he died the next day. After his funeral, I came back to the island where he died and where we lived together many years earlier. And I waited for him to show himself. I was so sure he would show himself. And he didn't. I went everywhere but he didn't; I saw nothing that was a message from him. Just before the funeral was happening, I also went back to a place where we sometimes walked, there were old, old stones, statues and things along the ocean, an incredible scenic place for walking. I said, 'Ingmar, Ingmar, please come back.' And I didn't hear anything. It was quiet, quiet, so I was very sad."

Liv noted afterward that she didn't mention her daughter's father's name initially during the interview because he is also "very famous" (film director Ingmar Bergman). She felt that the story was important because it is an example of Kevin's "incredible gift," regardless of the couple's fame. The island where they had lived together and where he had died was the Swedish Fårö island. Throughout the island there are limestone monoliths called "raukar" which originated during the Ice Age in Sweden. After he looked at Ingmar Bergman's picture, she recalled in the interview:

> "And then Kevin suddenly said, 'Oh, he is saying to you that when you went among those big stone foundations, he answered you. Maybe you couldn't hear him at the time.' There is NO way! He [Kevin] didn't know [about the islands with stone formations]. Ingmar answered me! Maybe he needed some years for me to really know he was there. I needed to hear it from Kevin, more than I would have liked to hear it maybe when I walked there. Because then I was so full of him anyway, I could have thought I made it up. It's incredible. I couldn't hear it then. He let me know years later that he did hear me. And he cared for me."

During a second reading, held at the home of a friend of Liv's, Kevin also mentioned to Liv privately, "There is a man here who passed away from leukemia."

"Yes, he was also a friend of mine," Liv replied.

She looked in her tote bag and said, "In fact I have a picture of him in here somewhere." But she couldn't find it at that moment.

"Were you looking at a picture of him recently and thinking he looked like one of the Kennedys?" Kevin asked.

"No," Liv replied.

"Are you sure?" Kevin asked again.

"No, I didn't."

"Well just remember I mentioned that."

Later that afternoon when he was done with the readings at this home, Kevin was relaxing with her friends on the deck. Liv exclaimed her appreciation in front of all that he had not only brought Ingmar to her at the last reading but also that day Kevin had brought in her close friend who had passed.

"I could have sworn I had his picture," she said as she rummaged in her tote bag again.

"Oh, here it is!"

Her friend asked, "Oh can I take a look?"

Liv handed her the picture. "Oh my God, he is so good looking. He looks like one of the Kennedys," her friend commented.

Liv screamed in surprise. The comment from Kevin was accurate, if a bit ahead of its time.

Alan, a forty-six-year-old data engineer, first mentioned in Chapter 7, described his gratitude for the confirmation from Kevin that his deceased parents are still with him.

During one of his approximately seven readings with Kevin over the years, Kevin asked Alan, "Is there something wrong with his [father's] hands?"

And Kevin held his right hand tightly clenched and showed this to Alan. Indeed, his father had suffered a severe stroke that affected his right side and he was unable to use his right hand. Alan noted in the interview that he had brought a picture of his father in good health, with a normal looking hand.

At the same house group reading, Alan's half-sister was being read and Kevin picked up that her father had engaged in an affair with a younger woman before her mother had died and they were still together now. His sister was amazed.

She responded, "Absolutely he had been [having an affair] and he thinks we don't know but we know!"

Later she shared with Alan, "I haven't told a soul about that; I can't believe he saw that!"

Also attending the same house party reading was the ex-mother-in-law of Alan's other sister. Kevin picked up that the baby she was raising was not her own and that the baby's mother had been a drug addict.

The woman agreed, "Yes and that was Alan's sister."

Alan's sister had died in her late forties from a drug overdose. Kevin also asked the same woman if her deceased husband had been working on a stone wall in her backyard.

"No, there's nothing like that," she replied.

Then Kevin asked, "Is there something wrong with the speaker in your car or your son's car?"

"No," she replied.

She didn't know what he was talking about. Later that evening she went home and mentioned these two odd comments to her son. Her son then told her the right speaker in his car wasn't working and that his dad had indeed been planning to build a stone wall in the backyard before he died and had talked to the neighbors about it as well.

Jeff Phillips, the husband of Brian, is professor emeritus at a research university and a semi-retired advanced practice psychiatric nurse who has provided psychotherapy and medication management for his clients for decades. Steeped in traditional Catholicism as a child, he converted to Buddhism as an adult. He has enormous respect for Kevin's ability and has had three readings with him in the past eight years.

On his first visit he brought a picture of his mother and a picture of himself with his siblings, three brothers and two sisters.

Immediately Kevin pointed to one of his brothers and said, "There's bad energy between the two of you. My suggestion is that you steer clear and this might eventually come around, but for now, I don't see this is getting better in the near future."

Kevin correctly picked up on their current estrangement and seven years later, the two brothers made amends before the brother died of cancer.

Next, Kevin pointed to one of his sisters. "She is a spirit, right?" [meaning she had died].

Jeff replied, "Yes."

Jeff described Kevin looking to the side and he said quietly, "Thank you."

Then he said to Jeff, "She's right here with me. She wants you to know she is free."

"That took me right out of the water as those were the same words my sister said to me, the last time I saw her, *I am free!*" Jeff explained.

Similarly, Kevin gave him a message from his mother, that were also her last words to him. Kevin also asked Jeff, "Have you got something wrong in your abdomen. Are you sick?"

Jeff, thinking he meant stomach and bowel issues said "No…oh but I was recently diagnosed with prostate cancer."

"Oh, that's what it is. I picked up an energy there but I didn't know what it was. Your mother wants me to tell you, - everything will be okay."

Those were also his mother's last words to Jeff before she died.

"You don't have to worry; she's got your back." Kevin told him.

Seven years later, his health status has remained stable in that regard.

Jeff walked out of his first reading, "Truly, emotionally I was just jolted, but there was a comfort in knowing that they are there."

During his second visit, Kevin spoke a lot of an upcoming new chapter in Jeff's life. Jeff mentioned, as others have noticed, that at each visit, Kevin did not recognize him from the last visit.

"So, it was as if each time I walked in as a total stranger. He didn't remember me and he just explained - I see so many people."

At this second visit Kevin asked Jeff, "I see students around you but do you do anything else?" Kevin asked him.

"Yeah, I do."

"You will really benefit from this new freedom. There's a whole new life ahead of you that's going to be a lot less stressful."

At that time Jeff was planning with some ambivalence to leave academia and go full time into clinical practice. Kevin assured him that the change he was contemplating was the right move and Jeff has never since regretted it.

Kevin commented, "There's someone in a leadership role that isn't good for you."

As Jeff was trying to think of someone within his department, Kevin immediately clarified,

"No, no, it's outside the department. She's new there, she's in a powerful role. Be careful of her."

Jeff then realized who this was in an administrative role within his college, "Boy did that one pan out, his insights were very much on point."

Kevin also spoke to his clinical practice, "You are not alone in those rooms...a lot of the work, a lot of the healing that goes on in there is partly related to the people around you." [meaning Spirits].

Jeff recalled that several of his clients have commented about "the spiritual energy in the room" or as one stated, "This place has good energy, I walked in the room and thought – wow!"

Kevin also brought in Carol, a dear friend and former nurse colleague of Jeff's who had passed, "She said it's about time [they made contact with each other]. She is really right there with you."

During that last reading Kevin also asked, "Is everybody okay in your family? I'm getting some energy changes in your family."

He didn't say someone was sick but he mentioned that a sibling would have energy changes. Jeff didn't understand this message until several months later when one of his brothers was diagnosed with terminal pancreatic cancer.

Lauren Torlone, introduced in Chapter 7, is a married woman in her thirties with two children. She is a writer and college professor. She first had a reading with Kevin ten years ago and has since come to know him as a friend as well. She has provided consultation on managing his online profile, ramping up his business, and managing his medium appointments. She loves to challenge him with questions about the afterlife as noted in Chapter 7.

Witness to the World Beyond   125

She recalled her first reading – she was with her mother. She was trying to get pregnant and asked him at one point, "Do you think I'm going to have a baby?"

"Did you recently have a miscarriage?" he asked. "Abortion and miscarriage look the same to me."

"No."

Her mom chimed in: "You just had a miscarriage about six months ago."

Lauren was not intentionally trying to fool him.

As she explained, "Oh my God, I had forgotten about it! I had moved past it; that was my coping mechanism."

Kevin did not say for sure what her future was in regard to children but he asked if she wanted to know the gender of the child that miscarried. She agreed. It was a girl. She would go on to have two healthy boys several years later.

Since that reading, Kevin has brought in many relatives, which gives both her and her husband great comfort. Lauren's mother-in-law has come through with love and affection for her husband. She also acknowledged his relationship with his living father could be challenging but to "go on and live your life…just let it go. He is a great grandfather to the kids."

Lauren's grandparents also have come through with support and gratitude. A grandfather named Jack Fitzgerald let her know through Kevin that he felt close to her husband, also named Jack. And that he was thrilled that they named their son Fitzgerald after him.

Her grandmother once admonished her through Kevin when Lauren and her sister recently had an argument, "This is so stupid. Life is too short." Lauren had not mentioned the spat with Kevin beforehand.

Lauren freely admits she is a Type A personality. Through her readings with Kevin, she has gotten help with various sources of anxiety.

As early as her first few readings with Kevin, he told her, "You are the highest functioning anxiety person; you have the best functioning anxiety and the worst, all in one."

Another time Kevin was reading Lauren in her bedroom, during a house party that she had sponsored. Everyone was having a private reading in this room. She was focusing on a blind that was bundled up, thinking her kids must have broken it.

Kevin broke through her lack of concentration with, "That blind is consuming so much of your mind right now because you are a perfectionist. You have to stop, it's crazy."

At times he has told her, "You obviously can control it [the anxiety]. I see you doing that now. You turn it on when you are bored for something to do."

Lauren admits, "I do think he has helped me a lot. It's powerful for someone to say you don't have any problems, but you can't expect your body to operate at one hundred percent for twenty-four hours a day for what – eighty years? That's not feasible. At some point you should probably stop doing that."

On a lighter note, Lauren recalled how her mother-in-law came through once about visiting her infant son.

Kevin told Lauren, "She's laughing that he has those spiderman pajamas on. Every time he wears them, she knows you didn't buy those. She loves to visit him in his crib in the morning. So, if you ever hear him talking and babbling in there…"

It has been a great comfort to her and her husband to hear this specific evidence that helps them to know that her mother-in-law is still in their lives on some level.

Chapter 11: Forgiveness, It's Not Your Fault

Tori, a twenty-nine-year-old woman who works as a marketing specialist and event planner, was aware of Kevin V. Coan's ability through her mother, a former client of his. Tori decided to bring her best friend Nina to see Kevin with her as Nina had lost her boyfriend and was still grieving. Their gang of friends had experienced a horrific tragedy during their senior year of high school. Tori had planned to go skiing with them one weekend but she had to change her plans at the last minute; Nina also did not go skiing that day as well.

While driving home after the day of skiing, the driver of the car filled with their friends started to swerve, reportedly due to low blood sugar. In the passenger seat beside him was Larry, Nina's high school boyfriend of several years, who tried to grab the steering wheel to stabilize the car. But in his haste, Larry overcorrected and the car flipped over on the highway. Larry lost his life; the driver and back seat passengers all walked away from the accident.

Tori and Nina walked into Kevin's office together approximately one year later. They put Larry's picture on the desk in front of them.

Tori recalled, "Right away he knew it [Larry's cause of death] was a head injury from a car accident. And right away he looked at Nina and said, 'Oh you guys were together.' Of course, we both burst out crying at that point."

Kevin then gave words of incredible comfort to Nina, who had been plagued with guilt and remorse about their last conversations via text – during that ride home. They were bickering about something minor; she had never shared this with anyone, including her friend Tori, that their final text conversations were a major source of regret.

Kevin told her, "Don't worry about your last conversation, that's not what was important. Larry doesn't care about that. He knows you guys were not being serious. That's not what anyone will remember the relationship by, it's not what he'll remember."

Having that kind of closure was so important for Nina, Tori acknowledged. Kevin also mentioned Larry's sister by name.

"Who is Erin? She is really struggling…. Larry's mom is not doing well herself, she has barely left her own bedroom, but she needs to remember that Erin needs attention too."

Kevin shared these observations from Larry's spirit who was concerned about this.

Kevin also mentioned Larry's infectious laugh and boisterous personality, which he was well known for, "Holy cow! I can hear him in my head – everything about him is just a lot of personality!"

And then he said to them, "What's this house that you're going to in Maine? You guys have to go on your trip, you have to celebrate Larry. He would want you to be together. He would want you to have fun."

Tori and Nina were once again shocked that he would know about this trip. They had recently planned to celebrate with a group of twenty-five friends at a house in Maine after their first year out of high school. But they were conflicted; it seemed too soon after Larry's death and several felt that they should cancel the trip.

At the reading, Tori shared, "It felt like he [Larry] was giving us permission."

And so, the group of friends went on the trip to celebrate his life and friendship as an integral part of their get-away.

Diane Grimaldi is an advanced practice nurse who has a private practice in psychotherapy and medication management. She met Kevin V. Coan approximately twenty-five years ago in his office and has since had about ten readings with him.

She recalled meeting him, "The first time I met him, I walk into the office and I didn't even get to sit down and he goes, 'Woah! I don't know who you are or what you do but everybody's emotional problems are all around you, all around you!'"

She decided to remain quiet initially during the reading as she didn't "want to give him any clues."

Kevin continued, "Well, all I can tell you is whatever it is you are doing, don't think for a second that you are doing it all by yourself. Because you are not. You are not alone doing this; you get a lot of healing light from others."

Witness to the World Beyond   131

Then he started to name family members that had passed, spirits that were helping her in her daily work of emotional healing.

Over time, Diane has occasionally recommended Kevin to some of her clients whom she thought would be open to the idea of a reading and could potentially benefit from it. She generally waits until six months have passed after the death of a loved one before she recommends him.

She tells them, "You don't have to believe in this, just go and take it in the spirit that it's meant to be and see what happens."

She then recalled, "Most didn't have high expectation but came away…as regular clients of Kevin."

For example, she had a client whose son died of an overdose.

Diane recalled, "She always felt guilty, like, what should I have done? What could I have done? I tried to help him but couldn't."

The message Kevin gave to her from her son was, "You did everything. There's nothing, nothing more that you could have done. This was going to happen no matter what you did. It had nothing to do with you. You are not responsible. You did more than most people would have done. And you stuck with me the whole time."

Marie, a retired woman in her sixties, is Kevin's friend and client. She met him approximately ten years ago through her sister who was friendly with him. Among the many stories she shared was one about forgiveness and the release of a lifelong sense of guilt. She had a friend in high school who had become involved in drugs and was having all sorts of problems.

Marie shared, "Maybe I was too young; it was just too much. I always felt like I sort of pushed him away and I felt bad about that. And then about a year or two after we graduated from high school, he passed away. It always bothered me, you know? I always wondered if my friend felt like I had turned my back on him."

One day when Kevin had stopped by to visit her for a social call, not a medium reading, Kevin noticed her yearbook on a shelf. He started flipping through it until he came to the picture of her friend.

He pointed to his picture and said, "You know what? He's not blaming you at all. You had nothing to do with anything that he went through."

Marie then shared in the interview, "I almost felt like somehow it wasn't Kevin speaking because I hadn't told him about it. I felt like I just could let it go, and then I let it go."

Paul M., a high school math and computer science teacher in his early fifties, shared his impactful first reading with Kevin when Paul was thirty years old.

When Kevin picked up his brother's photo at a group house party he asked, "Whose picture is this?"

Paul raised his hand and Kevin started his reading with, "Something about football? I'm hearing a game."

Paul said that didn't make sense although he used to play football on occasion with his brother when they were younger, being only three years apart.

Then Paul described the scene, "He [Kevin] starts doing this [Paul mimics Kevin's motion at the time of patting just above the right side of his forehead]. And he said, your brother just wants you to know that he's okay. He is all right, don't worry about him."

Paul M. explained that on December 16, 1985 at 8:30 pm. he had walked into their shared bedroom at home to grab his glasses while watching a Patriots football game against Miami with his father. Paul was sixteen years of age when he found his brother, dead by suicide, with a gunshot wound on the right side of his head. He explained:

"I will tell you, as you probably know, suicide leaves way more questions than answers. It leaves guilt, finger pointing, everything. So up until the age of thirty, almost for fifteen years of my life, there was guilt. Should I have said this? Did we not see that? And I had seen him earlier that day! I was close to him, very close to him.

So, it really hit me hard. You know it's almost like losing a twin. I now say to Kevin: You know you changed my life? You saved my life. That suicide answer...it's a box I can finally check off. You know I've been to therapy; I've written goodbye letters; they tell you to do that. I had done all that stuff but.... that lingering part was now finally gone [after the reading by Kevin]. Also, as I'm getting older too, I mean I don't want to die but I'm not so afraid of it now."

Candice, a nurse in her forties, met Kevin approximately fifteen years ago after being recommended to him six months after the sudden death of her father. She was living at home at the time and had not yet finished nursing school. Her father's unexpected cardiac arrest was shocking to the entire family. Her parents had a very strong marriage and her mother was devastated. Her husband (Candice's father) was fifty-three years old; he had just received an excellent health report from his doctor three days prior. He was not on any medications.

Every day Candice's father got out of work at the police station at five in the afternoon and was home by 5:15 pm on the dot. Even the dog lined up to greet him at 5:15 pm each day. One day he was late coming home. By 5:40 pm her mother started to panic and called his work. They told her that he had left at five o'clock per usual. He finally came home a few minutes before six o'clock.

"Where the hell were you?" her mother asked.

"I actually stopped at church on the way home."

"Why – did you have a bad day? Did something bad happen at work?"

Her dad responded, "I just felt like I needed to thank God for all the things in my life."

Candice said this was very uncharacteristic of her father to stop at church after work. He died later that night.

After her father's death, the family got a recommendation for a reading with Kevin and he agreed to come to their home with Candice, her mother and older sister present.

Candice recalled, "I was just so angry; I mean I wasn't really open to it. I was more there to be supportive of my mother. So, I had taken down all the pictures of my dad because people said he could look over your shoulder and say, 'Oh I see this person…"

Her mother did show Kevin one picture of her father.

Witness to the World Beyond   135

While Candice didn't remember all the specifics Kevin came up with during the reading, she shared her memory of it during the interview.

"I can remember being like – Did he look this up? How would he know all this information?"

As she was trying to process all that he was saying in that first reading, he suddenly turned his attention to her and said, "You don't believe me."

She admitted, "I don't."

He asked if he could talk to her for a minute to validate what he was saying and she agreed.

Kevin then said to Candice:

> "You were sitting in your car at the cemetery. But you didn't get out this day, you just sat in your car. An ambulance drove by and…something about this particularly company…it wasn't because it was an ambulance, it was because of whatever was on the side of the ambulance. You got so mad you said 'Fuck them for killing my dad.' And then you laid your head on the steering wheel and you cried. I just want you to know that your dad was with you."

"And that's exactly how it went!" Candice recalled during the interview.

Since that first reading, Candice has become friends with Kevin and has had numerous medium house parties for friends and acquaintances. She estimates that Kevin has read her personally over fifteen times. She shared a story about a friend of a friend that occurred during one of her medium house parties.

Kevin said to the man, who was unknown to Candice, "I'm just going to speak bluntly. I need you to know it's not your fault, it's not your fault. He's not dead because of you, it was going to happen anyway, it was an accident. You have to let go of that because it's not your fault."

The man "just lost it" after Kevin told him this. The man was in his fifties and later explained that he was in a car accident when he was seventeen with a group of his friends. After Kevin's reading, a lifetime of guilt had suddenly turned to a glimmer of hope and healing.

Scott Whitley, the TV/radio personality introduced in Chapter 7, also recalled observing a reading at one of Kevin's medium shows that Scott's station sponsored:

> "At one point he held up a picture and a young lady, I think she mentioned she was twenty-four years of age, stood up. Kevin started in immediately, 'It's not your fault.' She immediately started tearing up. Kevin mentioned, 'I see a highway.' She responded with the name of the highway but he said, 'No, don't tell me too much. It's not your fault. I see a highway. I hear an argument about his friends getting him back into drugs and alcohol. It's not your fault.' She started crying again at this moment."

After the show ended, Scott went up to the woman and asked if she minded sharing with him what the phrase "it's not your fault" meant to her.

She replied, "Well we were driving back home and we were arguing about his friends getting him back into drugs and alcohol."

She explained that she kicked him out of the car onto the side of the road on the highway. He was later struck and killed while walking along the side of the road.

Witness to the World Beyond   137

On a lighter note, Scott also witnessed a reading that spoke of forgiveness for a childhood mistake. During the course of one of these brief readings at an open restaurant medium show, Kevin said to one man, "You know they know about the fire in the barn." He was referring to the spirits from this man's family knowing this.

Scott recalled, "I saw the guy's face go white [laughs] and he goes, 'All right, I need to explain that. No one at the table knows [his family was with him] but when I was a kid, I accidentally set fire to the barn."

Liz Baker, a flight attendant, friend and colleague of Kevin's who has had more than twenty formal and/or informal readings by Kevin over the past fourteen years also recalled an observation at a restaurant show. After Kevin introduced himself, he explained his process of choosing one picture among the many that were put on a table at the front of the hall. At Liz's table, one of the younger women had brought a boyfriend that Liz didn't know.

He began snickering almost immediately as Kevin introduced himself, "Oh my God I can't believe this. Yeah, right, you talk to dead people."

At one point Kevin picked up a picture and showed it to the crowd, "This person is here."

So, the skeptical boyfriend stood up and said, "Yeah, that's my brother."

As he often does, Kevin only asked for his first name and the town he lived in.

Kevin began, "Your brother died by suicide."

Immediately the tone and response of the man changed as tears started down the side of his face.

"He wants you to know it wasn't your fault, he is happy now."

Liz recalled that the man later acknowledged that he had had an argument with his brother just before he killed himself. He has since carried that guilt with him all his life.

Kevin then continued, "You used to play with Star Wars toys when you were kids. You were up in the attic going through the toys last week. Your brother wants you to know that he was there."

Liz recalled watching the man as he "burst out crying. He was hysterical, could not contain himself. He walked out of the room an absolute mess."

Then he came back in later and thanked Kevin, "Oh my God I can't believe this, you know I carried this around." Liz commented in the interview, "Here's somebody that was just a mess, snickering, and now is like a one hundred percent believer. Absolutely."

Chapter 12: The Illusory Nature of Time

Kevin V. Coan does not consider himself a psychic. He clearly does not appreciate it when people ask him to predict their future or to give advice on betting; that is not his business. He also cringes when people refer to him as a "psychic medium."

"I don't pretend to be a psychic. Sometimes I get things for the future and whatever but…these people who claim that they're both, you can't do both and be good at it."

And yet, he often tells people, "Remember I said that…" when something doesn't quite make sense to them. He acknowledges that the information he receives from Spirit is not always linear; he cannot judge the time frame of the visions he sees or the words that he hears from beyond. This chapter details testimony regarding Kevin's ability to visualize the future at times as well as the past and present.

At a private house party reading, Kevin recalled that a woman waited to speak with him afterwards. He did not remember her which is a common occurrence for him, having read her years ago. The woman shared with Kevin that he had recommended that she not allow her husband to buy a motorcycle during a reading several years ago. The woman returned home after the reading and insisted that her husband not go through with his plan to buy a motorcycle. She almost managed to change his mind until her mother-in-law interfered. Her husband's mother scoffed at her beliefs in a medium and paid for the motorcycle herself. He died in a motorcycle crash within a few months of the purchase. The woman thanked Kevin for his efforts to try to stop this but wanted him to know the outcome.

Similarly, Kevin read another woman at a house party decades ago and asked about her younger living brother.

"Is he a golf pro?" Kevin asked

"Yes, he is."

"Is his health, ok? I can see that he is very, very sick."

"He's fine. He's healthy. He's only twenty-three-years-old!" she replied.

"Don't play God with him. Tell him he must go to the emergency room soon," Kevin warned.

The woman thought he was totally wrong on that call. She said nothing to her brother. Twenty years later, the woman came up to Kevin at another venue and reminded him of her story. She wanted him to know that three to four weeks after that reading, her brother had an acute liver infection and died soon thereafter. Nothing could save him. But if it had been picked up earlier...perhaps. She regretted not listening to Kevin but wanted him to know that she appreciated his attempt to warn her.

At times the ability to see into the future is not related to a highly charged emotional or heart wrenching story but simply speaks to a mundane vision in the near future. One day Kevin was at a friend's house with her daughter and several of her friends for a group reading.

At one point Kevin asked them all, "Does anyone know someone named Eliot?"

They all said, "No, no, no."

"Are you sure?" Kevin persisted.

Everyone again denied that they knew an Eliot.

"Well, Eliot, remember that name. Listen for the name Eliot."

After several hours of readings, Kevin was sitting relaxing with them all on the porch before he left. A car pulled up with an older couple in it.

The man got out of the car and asked the group, "Excuse me, is there an Eliot in this house?"

Kevin never found out who that Eliot was, but again, it was something Spirit saw coming, even though the reason behind it was never made clear.

Diane Grimaldi, the nurse therapist, shared what she at first considered was a "bad day" that Kevin must have been having during one of her readings. Nothing was making sense; it did not seem relevant or pertinent to her.

He asked her at one point, "How many people do you work with?"

She replied, "Nobody, I work by myself."

"Oh, I see you in a room…" and he went on to describe the room in detail, how it was laid out, the tables were round, how many were sitting at each table…and he saw that Diane was talking to hundreds of people.

She thought, "that's definitely not me."

Then Kevin asked, "What's wrong with your mother?"

"Nothing, why?"

"They [the Spirits] are showing me coughing, coughing...she's coughing. When she goes to a doctor, if they tell her, 'It's nothing, don't worry about it,' tell her she has to go back. And if she gets a new doctor at some point, you won't like this doctor. No, no, I take it back, you REALLY don't like this doctor!"

Again, Diane thought Kevin was having a bad day, her mother was fine and she couldn't imagine not getting along with her mother's doctor at any point.

She described herself, "I get along with everyone, you know, I'm easy."

Maybe he was getting his signals mixed up this day, he's "just off his game," she thought at the time. She called her mother later that evening and she was fine. Diane had no plans or ambition to speak at any conferences.

Several months later Diane was invited to give three lectures at what she thought was a small speakers' forum related to mental health issues. She hadn't connected it at the time with Kevin's reading until she entered the room and it was set up just as he had described. It was a much larger venue than she thought she had agreed to. There were over five hundred people there in her "breakout" sessions. Not being comfortable speaking to such large groups, she nonetheless managed to ace the talks and it helped to know that Kevin had foreseen this and that she was meant to do it.

Approximately six months after the reading, Diane was speaking to her mother on the phone when her mother started coughing. Again, she wasn't thinking of the past reading with Kevin initially.

Diane asked her, "What is the matter?"

Her mom replied, "Oh I don't know; I went to the doctor for it and he said it was nothing."

It all came back to Diane at this point. "You know something? You have to go back," Diane insisted.

"Why? I already saw him and he told me it was nothing."

"I'm just telling you; you have to go back."

Her mother obeyed her nurse daughter's directive and she was soon diagnosed with an inoperable tumor in her lungs.

Diane recalled, "This is exactly what he said. And it struck me because he doesn't usually tell you about things that are about to happen. He told me in private conversations that sometimes he doesn't have a time frame. I don't think he likes to tell people what's going to happen but sometimes he doesn't know if it has already happened or it is going to happen."

Diane smiled as she recalled the final prediction that came true:

> "So anyway, she ends up having this inoperable lung cancer. And she gets this nitwit for an oncologist. And I had the biggest fight with him that I had ever had with anyone because he was an idiot! He was rude to me and I was screaming at him. When I think about the whole course of my life, I don't think I've ever yelled at anyone like I did with him. I told him 'If I treated my patients like you do, I would be out of business!' And in the middle of it, all I could think of was Kevin; the session when I thought he was having a bad day, he's way off the mark. Every single thing he said happened, it was just like…later."

When Tori, introduced in Chapter 7, went for a joint reading with her friend Nina, Kevin also gave Tori some personal information that she thought didn't make any sense at the time. She was in the spring semester of her freshman year at college.

Kevin asked Tori, "Oh, you hate The New York Times?"

"What?" Tori responded with a puzzled look.

"You hate The New York Times and you are going to change your major."

"Nope, I don't read The New York Times, I don't read the news. I don't know what you're talking about," Tori replied.

In addition to her denial of any feelings toward The New York Times she had not contemplated changing her major in journalism.

Tori remembered him specifically saying, "Well, I'm not changing it. There's going to be a moment when you say 'I hate The New York Times' and you will know your grandfather is there. And he will be saying that it's okay if you change your mind and want to change your major."

One year later, Tori recalled that she was taking a very challenging journalism class for her major. The professor required the class to read The New York Times front to back every day and would randomly pop quiz them on it.

"I remember sitting back at my desk one day saying, Arghhh, I just hate The New York Times!"

And then she remembered Kevin's reading and thought, "Oh that's funny, hi Grampy, I guess you're here right now."

By that time Tori had also been thinking about switching her major in order to be able to have a study abroad semester. The journalism major would not allow it with its required strict schedule of on-campus courses.

Witness to the World Beyond 145

Until she vehemently uttered the words, "Oh, I hate The New York Times," she hadn't been thinking of her reading with Kevin a year prior. She decided to change her major to psychology with a minor in media studies to allow for the experience of a semester abroad. It had all worked out as Kevin had said.

Brian Phillips and his sister had a joint reading after their mother's death

Kevin asked the sister, "Well, you work from home?"

"No, I work in an office setting." [As an Internal Revenue Service worker, she was required to work every day in the office.]

"Well, I see you working from home a lot in the very near future."

"Am I getting fired?"

"No, you're not getting fired but you will be working from home. Just remember I said that, it may not make sense now but it will eventually," Kevin responded.

The sister just let it go, it made no sense to her. It was the Fall of 2019, several months before the world was aware of the COVID-19 pandemic.

Later, in the midst of the pandemic, his sister texted Brian, "Do you remember what Kevin said? I'll be working from home? I've been working from home for eight months now, I haven't even gone into the office."

Another "out of time" comment that Kevin said to Brian's sister was about her son.

Kevin asked her, "Now he's in school, right? College?"

"Yes."

"Well, I think he's going to take a year off."

"I hope not!" she responded.

"This is something you will be talking about as a family because that's what he's thinking right now."

Her son had not raised this issue at all at the time but indeed, it came to pass that within a year he took a year off from school after much family discussion.

Jeff Phillips, Brian's husband, also shared a future prediction that he received from Kevin. During his last reading with him, approximately a year prior to the interview, Kevin told him:

> "You're going to have some new property soon. You've been dreaming about this for a long time and it's going to come true. It's near water. It's what you've been looking for. I don't know where it is but this is something you've been looking forward to for a long time. It's going to happen. You just need to be patient."

At that point Jeff and Brian were just thinking about selling their home in Boston. On top of their list of locations was an island in Maine where Jeff had grown up during the summers of his youth. At the time of the interview for this book, things were still in flux and they were in a temporary rental on the mainland in Maine. It took over two years for Kevin's vision to be realized. Today they are happily living on the island in Maine where Jeff's original family has a long history since the early twentieth century. It was the realization of their dream and Kevin V. Coan's prediction.

Paul M., the high school teacher who shared the impact of Kevin's reading of his brother in Chapter 11, also shared a brief example of how Kevin's messages are sometimes geared toward the future. Kevin asked him during one reading if he knew anyone named Jordan. Paul replied he did not.

"Are you sure you don't know a Jordan? Well ok, but look for it. Remember I said that. When you are with a Jordan, your mother will be with you."

Sure enough, Paul M. was in Disney World with his partner several months later and it started to rain. They sought shelter near a beer kiosk in Epcot.

"Would you like a beer sir?" the waitress asked him.

"Sure, I'll have a Heineken," he replied.

He then noticed her name tag: Jordan.

"It's a name that just doesn't come up much, it just doesn't!" he exclaimed. He was happy to think that his mother was with him at that moment.

Elaine Simmons, a woman in her early fifties, lost her mother in January, 2014. Her father had passed only four years prior. She had known Kevin for approximately twenty years at that point and asked for a reading soon after her mother's death. She was grieving the loss of her mother immensely; she described feeling "unbearably devastated."

She described her relationship with her mother, "We were like best friends; we were inseparable. My husband always said that we were like two peas in a pod."

Elaine described how she did everything for her ill mother at the end of her life. She did her errands, paid her bills, visited her at assisted living every day despite working full time while running four restaurants. She would take her out to dinner in a wheelchair to all her favorite places.

Kevin advised her during one reading soon after her mother's passing, "Remember I said this. Your mother wants you to know about a yellow butterfly and when you see a yellow butterfly, she wants you to know she is there with you."

Elaine said she didn't know what he was talking about.

"Well just remember it," Kevin advised.

Six months later during the summer, Elaine recalled that she and her sister spent a day together relaxing by the pool:

> "And so, we are hanging out by the pool and this little yellow butterfly came up to me and was flying around me. I was like, 'this is weird, this butterfly won't leave me alone!' I hate to say it but I'm not much of a big nature person myself. Patty [her sister] was laughing at me. It landed on my face and was like kissing me and tickling me. I started laughing. I said, 'Oh my God, I haven't laughed since Mom died six months ago!' And it would not stop. It was tickling my face, tickling my face. And then it landed on my shoulder. And then I said, 'Oh my God, now I remember – Kevin said to remember this!' It lasted for like five minutes. I mean butterflies don't land on you! It was really incredible."

Alan, the engineer who was mentioned in Chapters 7, 8, and 10, recalled one reading where Kevin told him, "You're going to get a mirror with gold trim around it.

Witness to the World Beyond   149

You're going to inherit it." Alan thought to himself his mother was moving out of her home the next weekend but she didn't own any such mirror. During her yard sale that weekend, Alan noticed a tissue box made out of mirrors with a gold trim. He decided to keep it.

Wendy Golini, a restauranter in her fifties, first met Kevin in 1997. She is a mother of a large clan encompassing her three adult sons along with four adult children that she took in during their teen years after their parents had died. She also fostered many other children when they had no place else to turn. She has three grandchildren from her sons and up to nine "unofficial" grandchildren from the other children she has supported over the years. Wendy shared some quick validation stories about comments that Kevin said that would come true in the future as well as several involved stories that were akin to "a tapestry" being woven into many subplots that all came together in the end.

A quick validation story about a future focused reading from Kevin included one that he gave her during one of her personal readings.

Kevin commented out of the blue, "It's in the Wonder Women comic books. It's in the closet and it's not opened. It's where the baseball cards are."

Wendy G. had no idea what he was talking about. A few months later, she was in a frantic search for her son's birth certificate. She needed it urgently for some reason. As she was searching for it, she pulled out the drawer in her closet and she found it underneath the "Wonder Woman" comic books that she had saved.

"I will tell you all my successes in owning restaurants and the things that have come my way are because I opened up that energy because of Kevin," Wendy shared during her interview.

She recalled that he was spot on during the first reading with a message from her nephew who had recently died and Kevin had also described in detail what she had been doing earlier that day. Much of what Kevin said at that first reading made no sense to her at the time.

He advised her, "just remember that I said that."

It was a rather strange circumstance that led her to that first reading. Wendy's sister-in-law was hosting a medium party with Kevin; she invited Wendy to come. Wendy declined as she was very busy opening up another restaurant at the time. But the afternoon of the party, her own sister dropped by Wendy's home.

"What are you doing here?" Wendy asked.

Her sister replied that she had dreamt of their deceased brother the night before and she realized when she woke up, she needed to come over and watch Wendy's children because there was somewhere Wendy needed to be. Wendy described her family as "very intuitive."

As Wendy drove over to the medium party at her sister-in-law's house, her deceased brother's favorite song came on the radio. She had arrived early when a friend let her in while her sister-in-law, as the host, was having the first reading privately out of sight before the crowd arrived.

As people started to straggle in, they waited patiently for Kevin to come out after the first reading with the host. When he and her sister-in-law returned to the living room, her sister-in-law noticed her. She hadn't been expecting Wendy G. and greeted her with "Heyyy!" and a welcoming smile.

As a first-time host, her sister-in-law then asked Kevin, "So how does this go? Who's next?"

He responded, "Who's Wendy? I need to talk to her first."

As noted, Wendy G. described a story from her very first reading with him, as a "tapestry." She remembered it well because it was "life changing."

First, Kevin exclaimed during her private reading, "Well, you had a busy day!"

She acknowledged that she had certainly had a very busy day.

"I see you in a room and you're pointing to the walls and you're talking about colors and I see the color red and there's ladders. Who is Paul?"

Paul was the name of her husband as well as a new contractor. Indeed, she had been in the process of a major construction project as she was expanding into a new restaurant. She had supervised the work for most of the day and the walls had been painted red.

Wendy recalled, "He talked about the walls and sconces that I was picking out. Like they were very specific. He described the room as if he were in it."

While she hoped to hear from her deceased brother David, the first to come through was a nephew who had recently passed.

Kevin started laughing, "well, he's foul mouthed!"

Kevin was communicating with her nephew who was describing his own recent funeral. Kevin knew right away his cause of death and was very accurate in describing it to Wendy G.

Then he said, "You had a laugh at his funeral, didn't you? The laugh was on him. You're sitting in the limousine and the laugh is on him."

Wendy knew that it was her nephew who was coming through. He was a rough and tough kid growing up, "no angel," as she described him. Nonetheless she was close to him and would point out his bigoted ways to try to change him, to no avail, while he was alive.

Then Kevin shared, "He's wearing a green robe and has an accent so thick, you can't even understand it."

Wendy explained that the guest priest who said the somber funeral Mass in their Catholic church was dark in color with a very thick accent and wore a green liturgical vestment. No one could understand him.

Wendy had been talking to her nephew inside her head in the church, trying not to laugh, saying, "Well now I know that you're in heaven because you're letting me know your views on being a bigot were wrong."

After the funeral Mass she drove in one of the limousines with his closest friends.

"We got into that limousine and we burst into hysterics because if you understood this man, you would understand why God had the last laugh with him."

However, the main story of that first reading with Wendy G. that came to fruition over time had to do with the upcoming adoption of one of her three sons.

Kevin had seen something as he was communicating with Spirit early on in the reading and asked, "hmm, is one of your children not your biological child? Because you're getting a real hard time from a grandmother and it's not your or your husband's mother."

She acknowledged that was true; one of her sons was not biologically or legally hers but she had been raising him for years while he still had occasional contact with his own biological family that was extremely dysfunctional.

"But don't worry," he said, "now your brother [David] is coming through and he says there's a ticket, just the ticket you need and it's underneath a TV screen."

Next, Kevin asked, "Does someone have a problem with a tire on their car? What about a tooth?"

Neither of these two problems meant anything to Wendy.

"OK, just remember I said that but don't worry, everything is going to work out," Kevin assured her.

Fast forward to the next year. Wendy had been busy opening up a new restaurant. She and her husband were still raising their three sons, one of whom they had no legal rights to. They still called him their son and he referred to them as Mom and Dad. She had been friends with his biological father who had asked her to take the boy and raise him; the mother had signed her rights away and the biological father knew his household environment was not a safe place for the child to grow up in.

Wendy had worked out an arrangement that she and her husband would raise and support him while the biological father and grandmother could collect the welfare checks for him. It meant that the boy would go to school in the city where his biological family was in order for them to be able to claim him. Wendy drove him back and forth to school every day while he lived with Wendy and was part of her family.

At one point, when he visited his biological family, there was violence in the house and he was injured; from that point on she immediately started the legal process of petitioning for custody and years later, they officially adopted him. The grandmother fought her on this despite the unsafe conditions in the home which included drug dealing.

Wendy G. sought the advice of lawyers for an emergency court date to give her immediate custody. Her lawyer explained that he would need a $2,000 retainer as it would be an uphill battle since she was not a biological parent or relative. She was determined to never stop fighting for the boy whom she considered to be "her child." However, she was stressed to the limit by the initial and future court costs; she feared losing her restaurant, and losing her house. Even the $2,000 would be a challenge to find at that point.

As Wendy G. and her husband drove to the court house for the emergency hearing on assault and battery of her then custodial son, she was frantic not to be late. The stakes were high for the life of the boy she had been raising for years. Along the route to the court, a FedEx truck turned in to cut in front of her, blocking her view ahead. Then another FedEx truck came up along her left side and soon one on her right. She felt like she was being convoyed to the court. She didn't hit any red lights and arrived on time with a parking spot right in front of the court that became available as she arrived.

At the court, Wendy, her husband, their attorney, the biological father, and grandmother were present as well as a court appointed lawyer representing the child. The lawyer and judge were discussing the need for an emergency removal of the child until such time as a full investigation could be conducted. She recalled:

> "I started to become unhinged a little bit and my attorney was like, 'Calm down. You're going
> to get thrown out of court.' 'No, no, I can't have my child in a stranger's home! Please tell me where you are going to take him!' I started crying. I burst out, 'Your honor, I don't care if you put me in jail because I'm going to find out where he is and I'm going to sleep outside that house every night so he knows he's not alone.'"

Wendy's attorney was told to remove Wendy from the courtroom because of her behavior. Her attorney tried to console her outside the courtroom but to no avail.

The lawyer representing the child eventually came out of the courtroom and sat beside her and told her, "Mrs. Golini, it's going to be okay. Wendy, it's going to be okay."

Wendy G. lifted her head said, "How dare you be so familiar with me when you are taking my child away!"

The court appointed lawyer responded:

"You don't remember me? I'm Jan, pumpkin soup? You are Wendy from PAULI'S restaurant, aren't you? I'm a vegan; your chef was making a soup at the time and brought me some without cream. You and I had a beautiful conversation about how you are an advocate for domestic violence victims. You told me about your children and fostering other children. Remember I told you that I was an attorney? I became an attorney because I was in the foster system. I'm going to make you his foster mother while you fight for custody."

That day in court, Wendy G. won temporary custody of her then fourteen-year-old son whom she had raised since his early childhood. She got legal permanent custody of him a year and half later. They would later officially adopt him at age eighteen as it was his choice to wait until then in order to minimize hurt to his biological family.

To return to Kevin's first reading: the tooth, the ticket and the tire were all explained later that day. Wendy called in to her restaurant after the joyful news of the court hearing. All of her employees were in the know about the day's big event.

"I have him! I have my baby! This is the best day ever!" she explained to one of the servers.

"Yes, what a great day Mamma!" [the servers' affectionate name for their boss].

One server then proceeded to tell her that they had cashed in all the daily number lottery tickets that were kept in a drawer under a monitor screen that looked like a TV screen.

"You and Barry won five thousand dollars to split! And it's just as well because Barry went to the dentist after he broke his tooth. When he came out somebody had slashed his tires."

Barry got new tires, Wendy could now easily cover her lawyer's retainer, he never charged her a penny more, and she no longer needed to worry about her son's security. Everything worked out for the best just as Kevin had suggested months earlier, but in a cryptic message from her deceased brother that made no sense at the time.

Kevin called Wendy G. later that fateful day "out of the blue" to see how she was doing. They weren't really close friends at that point; he was not aware of the court hearing that day.

He started the conversation with, "How are you doing?"

"Great!" she responded.

"I just keep getting this and I have to ask you the weirdest question. Did you get cut off by a FedEx truck today?"

She laughed and responded, "Yeah, I was surrounded by them!"

He replied, "Your brother said he wasn't in your way. He was leading the way."

Witness to the World Beyond   157

As she shared this story during the interview, a FedEx truck went by her house as she sat near her window speaking on the phone.

She screamed while laughing, "Oh my God! A FedEx truck just went by my house! I'm not kidding! Oh God bless you, David!" [her brother].

Several years later, before Wendy G. returned to court to officially adopt her son, she had a reading where Kevin kept mentioning she would see black fuzzy dice at some point soon. Her husband drove her and the three sons to the courthouse that day. As he pulled up to the courthouse, there was a cab in front that had large black fuzzy dice hanging from the mirror. She pointed it out and explained that Kevin had seen it as some sort of a sign. They also had been "co-opted" by a FedEx truck again in the front of the court.

Next, she recalled, as they were waiting to enter the courtroom, "My son walks up to the concession area in the courthouse and there's a blind man that runs the concession. Hanging on his wall are black fuzzy dice. My son is laughing, 'Mom, there's the dice again.' There was a saying underneath it talking about God and family."

When they finally entered the courtroom, sitting on the judge's bench were several books with a pair of small black dice on top of them.

Chapter 13: The Cynics and the Skeptics

Kevin V. Coan is well aware of the critiques of mediums. He commented, "Those who use some form of trickery make the ones that are legitimate look a little bit bad, but at the end of the day, I've got people that have faith in me."

Over the course of his career as a medium, Kevin has run into many doubters. He recalled one of his very first readings that involved a woman who was "sort of hard as nails. I started in and I said - Oh she's going to be a tough one."

Right off the bat, she said to him, "Well, I'm a real skeptic."

He told her that was ok. She had lost her husband and through his connection, Kevin said to her, "Your granddaughter lives out in Seattle. I know she has a dream catcher in her room because your husband visits her in that room with the dreamcatcher."

She responded, "Oh my God, oh my God. I bought her that dreamcatcher."

Later she sent Kevin a phone message thanking him for coming to her house and for his kindness. He noted however that he has found that, in general, women are more open to the idea of mediumship than men.

Kevin's family members were also skeptics at times. As his own father lay critically ill in the Intensive Care Unit, Kevin, his mother and his aunt came to visit. The doctors desperately needed the information from a heart catheterization to determine the best plan of care but the procedure was deemed very risky in his condition. When Kevin, his mother and aunt arrived in the room, his father's brother was already there. His father was out of bed, strapped to a chair sitting upright, alive, but unresponsive.

First thing his mother asked her brother-in-law, "Gerry, have you heard from the doctors?"

"No, we haven't heard anything yet today," he replied.

Kevin announced, "Well they're going to do the catheterization tomorrow."

"Who told you that?" his uncle asked.

"The Spooks," Kevin responded.

His uncle had never been a believer in Kevin's ability and generally refused to even talk about it.

"What the hell is this mumbo jumbo? Look at your father. They would kill him in that condition."

"Gerry, I am not going to argue with you. All I'm telling you is that the doctors discussed it this morning and they don't want to put it off any longer."

Within minutes the doctors entered the room. One of them knelt down beside Kevin's father who, although he was not responsive – the doctor said to him, "Hi Mr. Coan. My name is Dr. Gold. Tomorrow morning we'll be doing the catheterization on you."

160 Barbara Ellen Mawn

The doctor then stood up and explained to Kevin's family, "We discussed it this morning. We don't want to put it off any longer."

His uncle never questioned Kevin again about his ability.

Kevin has also experienced people trying to trick him and prove that he is not legitimate. Two brothers had a competing radio show with the Pat and Scott Whitley program. These brothers came to one of Kevin's shows sponsored by the Whitley's radio station and had their secretary place a picture of a live person on the table up front as opposed to a person that had passed. Kevin ended up not choosing that picture but nonetheless they badmouthed Kevin on the air despite no evidence to substantiate their claims.

Kevin explained that it would not have mattered if he had picked up the live person's picture anyway – he often gets information from Spirit about a live person. Kevin does not appreciate such public attempts to repudiate his ability. His purpose is to "enlighten" not "convert" but he nonetheless enjoys the warm smile of surprise and acknowledgment of his abilities from a former skeptic.

As noted in Chapter 7, Shirley, the wife of Pat Whitley, a local radio and TV personality at the time, had heard of Kevin's medium abilities and invited him over to do a reading. As he entered their home, "…there was Pat with his arms folded across his chest and shaking his head." Shirley suggested that her husband Pat be read first.

Witness to the World Beyond   161

Looking at his body language Kevin thought Pat might be almost impossible to read. "If someone has that wall, nothing comes through."

Shirley said that she'd stay in the room because she knew Kevin could use her vibration even if her husband was blocked. Pat, the skeptic, had a picture of his mother Gladys with him. He assumed that Kevin would have googled him in advance and trolled information from the internet about him. Although Kevin usually would ask where the deceased person was from up front, he didn't this time as he sensed it was out of state.

Kevin started the reading with, "Well, Gladys tells me that when you were a little boy, you lived in Alabama right across the street from a German prisoner of war camp."

"I did!!" Pat responded.

"They let the prisoners out one day and they came over to your front lawn. They built a fountain in the front of your yard and you were looking at a picture of it this afternoon."

Pat was now astounded, "I was! How did you know that? No one knows that. That's not found anywhere!"

As his son Scott Whitley later recalled, that reading was "what kind of got my father interested in doing this [the sponsored medium dinner shows]."

As noted in Chapter 7, his father Pat contacted Kevin several years later to work collaboratively as a sponsor for some of Kevin's public medium shows, mainly in local restaurants. Pat has since shared with Kevin that he was a complete skeptic about mediums but "...you're the only one I respect." Today, his son Scott manages the radio station and continues to sponsor many of Kevin's public restaurant medium events.

Scott had difficulty during the interview expressing his understanding and acceptance of Kevin's ability. While

162 Barbara Ellen Mawn

he continually referred to his observations of Kevin's shows over the years as "amazing," he recalled feeling quite skeptical when his father first mentioned sponsoring Kevin's shows.

"I don't know...I don't really believe in it," he told his father. He was surprised that within twenty minutes of advertising the first sponsored show over the air, it was sold out.

He was tasked with hosting the first show but he went in with the attitude, "I really don't believe in it but that's all right. I'm gonna go in there and entertain and have fun. That's what my job is."

To this day that first show made a "dramatic impact" on Scott. Yet he seemed to have some confusion when explaining what he believes at this point.

Scott shared in the interview, "I always tell Kevin, I'm never going to believe, I'm never going to believe. But man, I see every single show and he gets every single person. It's the most amazing thing I've ever seen. He'll say things about that person when he's doing a reading that only they would know."

Scott emphasized that Kevin has never asked for a list of names that registered for the shows, nor would Scott have ever offered it in any case. There was never any way that Kevin could have googled anyone in advance.

Scott has described Kevin's ability as, "almost scary, especially when he's really, really targeted, if somebody is giving him feedback. I don't understand it, but there are certain people that have higher energy maybe?"

As a radio and television producer himself, Scott noted that with editing technology today, "You can make anybody look great by creative editing. But when you go to one of Kevin's shows live, you're like ...that's not edited!"

Witness to the World Beyond   163

Scott recalled many additional brief snippets of readings that have made an impression on him. One was a couple whose son had passed away in a car accident.

Kevin said to the couple, "I just keep hearing this song in my head, I just keep hearing it." [Kevin named the song at the time.]

Scott recalled that the parents immediately said, "He passed away a couple of weeks ago. We went to where they towed the car and they had ejected the CD. That was the only song on the CD."

At times there has been some levity in the course of Kevin's readings. One time during a restaurant medium event, Scott recalled:

> "It was an older woman, she had to be in her eighties. Kevin starts reading the picture of her husband who had passed away. She was a little bit…sourly, a little edgy. So, Kevin starts talking about him as a very friendly person.
> 'People said he should be the mayor,' Kevin told the woman.
> And she's like, 'No!'
> 'But I can see him talking to everybody…'
> 'Well, he NEVER talked to me!' she complained.
> Kevin changed his tact a bit, 'I see him sitting in this lounge chair at night.'
> 'Well, he was a lazy bastard!'"

Scott smiled as he mentioned, "That got the whole place rolling."

Scott commented that readings "involving kids are the toughest." At one reading after Kevin picked up the picture of a young girl, age seven or eight, the father stood up but immediately sat down, he just couldn't stand up anymore despite his family by his side at the table. Kevin continued the reading nonetheless. He started out by talking about their former dog – and identified it correctly as a golden retriever.

"They had a different relationship than a regular pet, they were very, very close," Kevin told the family.

"Yes," the father acknowledged.

"I just want you to know the dog is there with her now, watching over her."

Scott noted, "that it is tough when you see the emotion of the family at times. But ninety percent of them are kind of uplifting. It's almost like they hear a message that gives them closure or hope."

After discussing several examples from his observations of Kevin's public readings, Scott shared, "These are the things I see on a regular basis that just, I don't know, like I said if there's a trick, I've seen a million of them and I can't figure it out. They're so detailed. It's absolutely amazing at times."

Scott has used other psychics and mediums for his sponsored shows but he always measures them against Kevin's ability and he generally concludes, "Yeah, it's just not Kevin." Scott has his own reputation to maintain and with Kevin, "It's a guarantee."

Scott has observed that some people start to shake as Kevin is reading them at the shows but he explained:

"By the end of the readings, he really puts them at ease because they're getting something that they maybe felt they've missed or lost or didn't get to say or experience. He can describe those moments in time that they're with you and I think that is reassuring to a lot of people."

Despite observing approximately one hundred shows over the past eight years, Scott said he was afraid to have a reading himself.

"I don't know what he could tell me but I'm too chicken."

Yet he likes doing the shows "because of the stories…not being read [myself] but because I like hearing the stories…I can't explain it, but it is truly a gift."

At one of the Whitley shows one woman was rudely heckling Kevin throughout the show. It annoyed him but he didn't want to interrupt the flow of the show so Kevin did his best to ignore her. The thought crossed his mind that she thought she was a medium and was trying to discredit him for whatever reason, jealousy perhaps. During the break half way through the show, several men in the audience came over to Kevin to complain about her behavior.

"I hope you don't read her!" one of the men said.

"Trust me, I have no intention of paying her any more attention than she is already seeking," Kevin responded.

The readings got underway after the break and Kevin picked up a picture of a deceased relative of one of the other participants and told the woman that, "He was a bookie."

"Yes!" the woman responded.

"Anyone could have said that," the heckler chimed in, interrupting the reading.

As Kevin later recalled, "I was so irritated with her by then, I asked the Spooks which picture was hers. They showed me; I picked up a small picture of a man. And sure enough, the heckler now stood up to claim that was hers."

"He was killed on a motorcycle and he wasn't wearing a helmet," Kevin began the reading.

The heckler woman quietly shook her head yes.

"And the motorcycle was ruined but was later reconstructed by family members. It is heading out to California now," Kevin continued.

The now subdued woman quietly acknowledged, "Yes, my son reconstructed it and it is showing at a Harley-Davidson show in California."

She kept quiet for the remainder of the show.

After the show, the men who had complained at the break about her asked Kevin, "Why did you pick her?"

"Well, I put her in her place, didn't I?" Kevin asked. They smiled and agreed. Whether she was a cynic or a jealous fellow medium he never knew, but she was a believer in his ability by the end of that show.

Alan, whose stories were mentioned in several prior chapters, is a data engineer and as such, holds a very much evidence-based perspective. He recalled the story of his first reading with Kevin "that made my jaw drop. I mean I couldn't believe it!" His friend Paul was having a group of friends over for dinner at his home followed by readings by Kevin. Alan really didn't believe in mediums at the time but said he'd keep an open mind and thought that it would be a fun evening in any case.

"My thoughts were: death is death, it is a black hole and there's nothing afterwards," he explained. Alan arrived a skeptic but soon felt otherwise.

"It was just very surreal from the beginning."

That morning Alan had been searching for a good picture of his maternal grandmother to bring to the reading.

The first thing Kevin said to him when it was Alan's turn to be read was, "So when you were looking through your photo album this morning, looking for a picture of your grandmother, did you come across a picture of yourself and say out loud, *Well, that's a really ugly sweater?*"

Alan told him, "No, I said that's a really ugly sweatshirt," when looking at an old photo of himself.

"Same difference," replied Kevin.

Alan exclaimed during the interview, "He took the words practically right out of my mouth! Could that have happened if he wasn't a medium? Would he have had to have some kind of recording device and was going around following people and implanting things? I was like I can't believe that! And from then on it was just like hit after hit after hit."

Alan had brought a date to the dinner reading and of course there was no way the host or Kevin knew who he was. Kevin honed in right away with him as well, "Did your brother live above the garage on a mattress because he had drug problems?"

Kevin was spot on with Alan's date about several other things as well. Alan's friend said, "I can't believe this just happened!"

As he was wrestling with how Kevin could have had this information, Alan rationalized that even if Kevin had been recording in Alan's own home somehow, he did not know that this guy was coming. By the end of that first group reading with Kevin in 2008, Alan wanted to go to every single subsequent medium dinner party. He was no longer a skeptic.

Brian Phillip's sister was initially skeptical of the whole medium world but had gone for a joint reading by Kevin with her brother at Brian's urging. The prediction about working from home, described in the previous chapter, obviously seemed as far-fetched to her at the time as the possibility of her son quitting college for a while. But at one point in the reading, Kevin said some things that he'd have no way of knowing unless his ability was real.

He described her son's personality and his relationship with his girlfriend right on target and then there was this, "Your husband is in a managerial position and just had a difficult conversation with somebody and had to let them go."

She was floored by this as she acknowledged, "As a matter of fact, when I was sitting in the car ten minutes before I came in to see you, my husband called and related that this had just happened."

Brian's sister left the reading, more perplexed than skeptical. "She was quiet, not critical, but not fully convinced," Brian said afterwards.

While Kevin had nailed many things about her mother's life, his sister didn't understand many of the points he made about her own life. Over time, with the emergence of the pandemic and its impact on her work and her son's decision to leave college, she lost her cynicism and realized indeed that Kevin had been correct during the reading about these future events.

Brian and his sister had been raised in a home that followed a strict Baptist religion. They hadn't been given an opportunity to contemplate, let alone accept, this type of communication after death. A year later, after several of the comments had come to pass, she was appreciative and acknowledged Kevin's ability.

Witness to the World Beyond 169

The husband of Candice, the nurse introduced in Chapter 11, was also a skeptic about the ability of a medium to connect with those who had passed. When they were first dating, Candice invited her then boyfriend to her mother's house where Kevin was coming to give readings.

Her husband wanted no part of it. "No, I don't believe in any of that stuff."

She insisted that he just do it for her sake. He reluctantly agreed

The first thing Kevin said to him was, "Your dad is here and he is being sarcastic. He is telling me to say hello to the altar boy."

Her husband had been an altar boy but was a pretty "fresh" kid as a young boy and so it was an inside joke from his father being called an altar boy.

Her boyfriend looked over at Candice as if to say, "How the heck did he know that?"

Next Kevin started naming several people who had passed in his family. Her boyfriend was getting overwhelmed and at one point didn't recall one of the people that Kevin was referring to. Later his family recognized that person as his grandfather whom he had not seen alive since he was five years old.

At one point during her future husband's reading, Kevin said, "I'm just going to lay it out there. Who's Tommy?"

"My uncle," Candice's boyfriend responded.

"It wasn't an accident. I feel like he was pushed," Kevin told him.

The back story that Candice revealed during her interview was about an uncle that no one ever talked about. He had been a very wealthy and successful man whose life had spiraled downward after getting into trouble with drugs and alcohol. He died after allegedly "falling down the stairs."

However, it was known that the uncle had met a woman who was also on drugs and who happened to have him sign over all his assets to her two days before he died. The girlfriend first called the police to report the fall. They found him dead on arrival at the foot of the stairs. The girlfriend was actively taking drugs when they arrived; they found her lethargic and confused. She was taken to the hospital and was promptly revived. She signed out against medical advice from the hospital shortly after regaining consciousness. She took control of all his money and they never heard from her again. Candice's husband, a policeman who was never a believer in mediums or anyone claiming psychic powers, is now a believer in Kevin's ability.

Paul DiCenzo, a married man, father of three grown children and five grandchildren, works full time as a lead data engineer and database developer. He had heard about this book being written and decided that he wanted to see Kevin V. Coan, a first such experience for him. He had considered visiting a fortune teller or psychic in the past, but never gave it the time. This time he decided what the heck, he'd find the time and make an appointment. He still missed his father who had passed away decades ago and thought it might help with his prolonged grieving process.

At the first appointment with Kevin V. Coan, Paul thought he didn't look like a medium. But he laughed in the interview as he added, "But then again, if you asked me what a medium looked like, I wouldn't be able to describe it."

Witness to the World Beyond   171

There were many things that Kevin told him that first session that made him wonder, "How could he know that?" First of all, his description of his father was "spot on" and not just in the physical sense, as he could have taken that from the pictures of him that Paul brought.

Kevin, as is his custom, did ask where his father had grown up and lived and worked. He described Paul's father as "a man of integrity…he gets involved in things…. he holds people accountable for things; he was well respected."

Kevin asked if Paul's father worked for the union and later moved into management. These were both correct statements about his father's employment history. Kevin also mentioned that Paul's father said that he thought Paul's retirement plan was the right thing to do. Paul did have a plan but hadn't shared it with Kevin or his father.

Kevin said of his mother, who had died four years prior, "Your mother was a very stubborn woman. She didn't like people to do things for her. She wants to thank you for taking her out so much and taking her out for ice cream."

Paul acknowledged that all of these descriptions of his mother were true. After his father died, at one point his mother got into a serious car accident after passing out while driving.

He recalled, "We never got her car fixed, took away her license. She didn't like depending on people to take her places but we had to. I used to take her out for bingo on most Saturday evenings and often on Sunday for ice cream. I don't know how he knew that."

At one point looking at a family picture, Kevin said, "I can see by this picture that your mom and dad were always together. They were inseparable. I don't think you and your wife are as close to each other as your dad and mom were."

With a long and successful marriage for over four decades, Paul took umbrage at this comment initially.

Kevin clarified, "I don't mean you are ready for a divorce or fight all the time, I just mean you don't have the same type of relationship that they did."

Paul then acknowledged that Kevin might be a bit accurate on that as he noted, "I'm not sure anybody in my family has the same relationship as my parents did."

In the first reading, Kevin also asked while looking at a family photo if Paul's son-in-law worked with his fingers.

"I don't mean mechanically; I mean I see numbers all around him. Does he work with numbers?"

"Yes, he did," Paul acknowledged as he was a marketing director for a company and was responsible for all the marketing budgets.

Again, Paul thought at the time, "Why did you pick him?"

Kevin also looked at one of his granddaughters and said, "This little girl is very sensitive but she's a very smart girl. Her parents are going to have to make a decision about what to do with her school."

Kevin also pointed to a grandson and commented that he was also sensitive, smart and capable but his parents would have to push him a bit in school as his interests would lie elsewhere.

Kevin asked Paul if he knew anyone who was in the Navy. "I see somebody with a navy uniform on… and he wants to say hello to you."

Paul responded that he had four uncles who had since passed that were in the Navy but recently, he was at one of their son's homes for a fiftieth wedding anniversary

Witness to the World Beyond   173

party. Paul thought it was most likely that cousin's father as they were talking about him.

Paul had lost a sister four years ago and she also came through in the reading.

Kevin said about her, "You and your sister at one point were very close but when she was passing and very sick, you really didn't communicate with her as well as you wanted to."

Paul acknowledged that this was somewhat true.

"She wants to let you know that's okay, everything's good here."

After this first session with Kevin, Paul was overall amazed and admittedly "very emotional." He recalled going around and telling people, "Wow this guy's pretty good news! He's right on."

He was disappointed however when he got home to find that his recording of the visit on his phone had gotten disconnected when he showed phone pictures of his children to Kevin at one point. He couldn't recall all that Kevin had said about his own children but he did recall quite a bit of the session. He was anxious to go back and get more. So, he scheduled a second reading within the next month.

Kevin does not generally recall what he tells people in readings and, as previously noted, often doesn't recognize people at subsequent readings. This threw Paul off immediately as Kevin occasionally said some of the same things about people that he had said a month ago without realizing it. Paul managed to record this entire interview and had printed notes from it which he referred to during the interview.

Kevin told Paul repeatedly, "Don't worry about it...your mother is looking after you," or "Your father is proud of you and your kids."

During the second session, Kevin paid a similar compliment about his father's integrity, "Your dad could make a deal on a handshake with someone and always honor it."

Kevin also said that the upcoming Christmas would be a big celebration this year. Paul was a bit skeptical of this as his family always celebrated Christmas and if things went well with the upcoming planned medical events in the family, "Yes of course they would," he thought to himself.

Kevin could see a big change was coming for one son and when Kevin looked at his daughter in a photo he said, "She's doing something special for someone and your father wants to let you know he's very proud of that."

Indeed, Paul eventually shared with Kevin that his son had an upcoming kidney transplant that he'd hopefully receive from his sister who was an excellent match.

Looking at a family picture Kevin asked which of the women had a problem with their midsection. Paul explained which daughter was giving the kidney to her brother; he wasn't sure if that was what Kevin was referring to.

Then Kevin pointed to his other daughter, "What about her?" Paul explained she was pregnant and was undergoing treatment for breast cancer.

Kevin looked at a picture of Paul's brother and asked if he has a truck, van or good size SUV. His brother who happens to be a brilliant scientist looked "like a hippie" in the picture. Paul thought at the time that perhaps Kevin was basing this question on his appearance.

"But yes," Paul acknowledged "he used to have a truck and then ten years ago bought a large Hummer."

Paul recalled that the second reading was even more emotional for him than the first reading. He also acknowledged that it was a very challenging time in his life with all that was going on within his family.

Paul D. concluded that he thinks that Kevin is "very good at what he does." But he still could not process how Kevin could actually receive communication about a living person from a picture let alone communicate with the dead.

And yet, when asked if he would ever recommend him given his concerns, he responded:

"I would refer people to him. I would. I think he could do people good if they believed certain things. I mean maybe those things are true, I don't know. Personally, I am skeptical. There could be some benefit there. I think it was well worth going to. I'm glad I had this experience. I definitely enjoyed it and learned a lot...and not just learning to be skeptical [small laugh] but I learned a lot and it also made me, you know, in my quiet time, think a lot more too on different things."

In a follow up conversation, Paul commented that the benefit he sees in mediums is that they can act like a life coach for some people but he remains skeptical about the ability of anyone to communicate with the dead. He does feel thar during periods of meditation or dreams, the subconscious mind can take over and help work on one's emotional issues. It is only within these times he believes that it may seem that one is in communication with the deceased.

Paul M., the high school teacher whose stories were shared in Chapters 7, 11 and 12, started out as a skeptic before his mind was changed at his first reading around 1997.

He explained that he was taking a self-development seminar course and one of the other students said to him, "You seem like you are open to stuff. Would you ever want to do a séance? I know a guy and you'd have to get some friends over."

In his mind he thought, "Dude you're crazy!" but nonetheless he agreed.

"So, I got ten of my kooky friends together and said some guy's coming over to talk to the dead. Fifty bucks, come on over! You've got to bring a picture."

They asked, "Do you know this guy? Who told you about him?"

"No, I don't know him. Some kook in a seminar told me about him…he'll probably be in some wizard hat…we'll just make a time of it!"

As Paul M. recalled in the interview with a smile, "I did NOT believe in this stuff. I didn't know why I did it."

Paul M. remembered that he was quite surprised to see Kevin when he arrived at the door.

"Who's this Irish accountant?" Paul thought. "Where is the wizard hat and cape?" he laughingly recalled during the interview.

His opinion changed quickly as Kevin read several people accurately. Paul had warned his friends not to tell him anything… "tell him lies even so he won't be able to take hints from what you say."

Kevin started the readings that evening with the host, Janie, who was Paul M.'s coworker. She had never met Kevin and was not "in cahoots" with him. Paul heard her saying 'yes' over and over again to questions and comments during Kevin's reading.

For example, Kevin told her, "You were just recently laying out a rug and your grandmother was there with you."

"Yes," she agreed, "the rug we are on at the moment when I was getting ready for this today."

Next, Paul's friend, Todd, raised his hand when Kevin picked up his deceased cousin's picture. Kevin said, "Your cousin thinks his wake was really odd…weird, more of a celebration of life…was there a band there?"

"Yeah, there was!" replied Todd.

At that point, Paul M. recalled thinking, "Now wait a minute!!!"

Later that evening, Kevin would give Paul M. a reading, the story shared in Chapter 11 about his brother who had killed himself with a Patriots football game on TV in the background.

Paul M. was astounded after his own reading and called Kevin the very next day. He recalled speaking with him for almost two hours asking him, "How did you know this?" How did you know that? How do you have this talent?"

Kevin patiently explained how his mediumship worked to Paul but then, perhaps worrying that this guy was going to be calling him a lot, Kevin mentioned, "some people are crazy and get addicted to this stuff and they want to do two or three readings a year."

Paul M. laughed as he recalled in the interview that he was ready to ask him to come back that night! He has become friends with Kevin over the past twenty-five plus years since then and has had over fifty readings, many of them sponsored in his own home with friends. His cynical

178 Barbara Ellen Mawn

view on mediums was eradicated after that first public reading.

Liv Ullmann, whose story of comfort and peace from one of Kevin's readings was described in Chapter 10, did acknowledge that before she first met Kevin, she had some doubts. While she believed that it was possible for a person to have legitimate medium abilities, she was leery of the plethora of people out there advertising these skills. She feared that she would be "googled" and it would be information available on the internet that the medium would present. At one reading at her home, she was surrounded by two of her Norwegian girlfriends who were both skeptics.

"Everybody had a time with him. My girlfriends were skeptical and probably that colored off a little on me. But I liked very much what he had said and thought…Oh yes that could be so, my mother is talking to him or my father."

However, at the first reading with him the evidence Kevin gave to her about her conversation with her former partner Ingmar Bergman convinced her that, "There is no doubt as to the higher power or someone that is out there who has left the world and has spoken to Kevin. It is a gift because I've seen it and I know it."

Kevin recalled a reading with a woman that he had given at a house party in a suburb of Boston. During the course of the reading Kevin told her that her grandmother had come through and she was showing Kevin that the woman was pregnant.

Witness to the World Beyond 179

"It is an impossibility for me to get pregnant," the woman responded.

"Well maybe you are soon going to adopt a baby? All I see from your grandmother is a baby in your arms and I'm pretty sure it's yours." Kevin replied.

"No, it can't happen," she again insisted.

She later went home and told her husband. They scoffed with a sad laugh at Kevin's expense because of the seemingly foolish vision he reported.

A few weeks later the woman called Kevin and asked, "Do you remember me? I was the last one you read at the house party in Billerica and you told me I was pregnant. I told you that was impossible."

"Yes, I sort of remember you now," Kevin replied.

"Well, I haven't been feeling well and I went to the doctors yesterday and I am pregnant!"

She explained that after she got the news, she was ecstatic and went to the car dealers where her husband works to tell him. He left work early and they drove into their driveway in separate cars behind each other. She then shared the next odd part of the story:

> "We were driving into my driveway where we have a wooden fence on one side of the driveway. It was late afternoon. On the fence in perfect lettering was a large XXOOO [hugs and kisses sign] with a bright light shining on the fence. My husband and I got out of our cars and stood there and stared at it for over twenty minutes before the letters and the light disappeared on their own!"

Kevin never heard from her again but one day while doing readings in another home, a woman introduced herself as the sister of the woman that he had read who

180 Barbara Ellen Mawn

thought she couldn't get pregnant and later found the XXOOO mysterious sign on her fence the day she learned of her pregnancy. They had a healthy baby girl, her sister reported.

"My sister told me to tell you that her husband is no longer laughing at you and neither is she!"

Wendy Golini, whose "tapestry" story of her son's custody was described in Chapter 12, shared two stories about observations of cynics at medium parties in her home. A friend of Wendy's who believed in Kevin's ability came to her home for a medium party one evening with her husband Mark. Mark was not there for a reading however, as he thought it was all nonsense. He was loud and demanding when they arrived, a "big, strong union man." He asked immediately if his wife could be read first as they planned to go out for dinner afterwards.

His attitude was obviously, "This is bullshit, can we go eat dinner?"

Mark's wife wasn't the first to be read as it turned out and Mark was forced to sit and listen to other people's reactions to Kevin's open group readings. By breaktime, Mark asked, "Can I get a reading? Can I get in on this?"

He paid up as required and when it was his turn Kevin started with, "Your father is standing here and he is front of a rose garden. He's got a little dog, a poodle with him."

At this point, the strong, cynical, tough guy lost it. "He started bawling his eyes out, like a baby."

Wendy G. still laughs about his quick conversion to belief in mediums because "he was such a ruffian, you know?" Kevin also offered him insights into his father's approval and appreciation of Mark's decision to take over

Witness to the World Beyond   181

the family business and his ability to make it profitable despite the challenges in the economy during that time.

Wendy also shared another observation of a cynic-turned-believer at one of her home parties with Kevin. A friend of a friend of Wendy's, named Joan, had come with several girlfriends just to observe but not for a reading. She wasn't a believer but presumably thought it would make for a fun evening.

She became "bowled over" observing Kevin's accuracy with others as he demonstrated with one woman by saying, "I can see your daughter [who had passed], she's in her wheelchair and she's blowing bubbles and the dog's jumping up and popping them."

The woman had tears running down her face, "Oh my gosh that's what Carolyn used to do!"

Although Joan seemed anxious to leave since her arrival, she said, "OK I want to get read." during a break.

The first thing Kevin told her was, "Your mother-in-law is coming through. She says she understands. It is not easy being with her son. I'm being brought to a 99 Restaurant in Haverhill, MA."

"What?" Joan asked incredulously.

At this point Wendy observed that Joan was just kind of staring at Kevin and not saying anything. She then looked to the left and to the right at her friends.

Kevin told her, "I don't know what that's all about but… she understands. Now I'm being brought to Kitty's Restaurant in North Reading. And oh, …aren't you late for something?"

The girl started to freak out Wendy recalled. She looked at a friend and said, "You told him! You told him!"

"I didn't f'ing say a thing! What are you talking about?" the friend replied.

Wendy later found out that this woman was having an affair. She had first met her lover, a bartender, at the 99 Restaurant in Haverhill, MA. She was indeed "late" for something that evening of the reading because she had intended to skip out early and meet her lover at Kitty's Restaurant. She had told her husband that she was going to this medium party for the evening as an excuse to pursue the affair.

In this case, the cynic turned into a believer but it was a stressful induction to mediumship indeed. Wendy G. commented that this was also an example of how Spirit does not embarrass people in public. It was never publicly stated that she was having an affair, this was personal information only she and one friend knew at the time of the reading. Kevin did not know what the communication from the mother-in-law meant; he was merely sharing the message that he had received.

Jennifer and Jake, first mentioned in Chapter 7, are a married couple in their early sixties with two grown children and one grandchild. They live in a coastal town in northeastern Massachusetts. Jennifer met Kevin V. Coan ten years prior at a girlfriend's house party. Jake did not attend. It was the only reading she has had. She shared her initial doubts about going. She had never gone to fortune tellers, psychics or mediums as she didn't believe in any of it.

"First of all, I am typically a very cynical person, so I was skeptical that any of this would be real," she shared in the interview.

Jennifer had taken detailed notes during her reading and referred to them throughout the interview. When she returned home that evening after the reading, she shared with her husband Jake what Kevin had told her. She noted that some parts of the reading did not seem relevant and some of it was uncannily accurate.

"But I was blown away by how many things he hit on," she said.

Jake described himself during the interview as a "nuts and bolts guy."

"I read one hundred percent nonfiction. If it doesn't happen, it doesn't matter to me. I'm in the mortgage business; I'm a numbers guy."

Jake had never really considered what mediumship might entail despite being vaguely aware of "all these silly people that give readings." He recalls he was "frankly mesmerized" after discussing Jennifer's reading for forty minutes after she came home that evening. He was the one to put many of the unclear pieces together.

Kevin began the reading discussing Jennifer's current job. He didn't know where she worked or what kind of work she did; he didn't ask.

Instead, he started the reading with, "I see all points north. The exit is a hospital exit. A lot of people are going to lose their jobs, I see a lot of boxes, as the company is moving. You won't lose your job but are going to have to think about whether you want to stay with the company."

At that time, Jennifer worked for a large global company at a branch in New Hampshire. None of the workers were aware that there was a plan to downsize at that time. There would soon be a massive layoff as Kevin predicted and those who retained their jobs, including Jennifer, would be relocated to an office in Massachusetts. She had never noticed that the exit she took every day for ten years had a hospital exit sign as well.

Both Jennifer's parents and a brother who had passed came through in the reading. Jennifer was only seven when her older brother had died in a car crash. During the reading, her brother showed Kevin her playing golf in Ipswich, MA, and sent along a tease about her golf game. Her brother chided her that she was never going to get much better at golf. She laughingly acknowledged that truth during the interview.

Jennifer's brother said through Kevin that he wasn't driving the car on the day he died but that, "it doesn't matter, it's nobody's fault…it was all in the past."

At the time of the crash the other person in the car, her brother's friend, survived. His friend was responsible for the accident, as the driver, but at the scene of the accident, the friend's father, a local police chief, reported that Jennifer's brother had been driving. Kevin had also seen that her brother had been decapitated as well. That was not reported to the parents at the time; only three people knew about it. When they later got access to the files, this indeed was how he had been found at the scene.

Kevin also shared that Jennifer's brother was calling her "a little squirt." She teared up in the interview as she recalled the first time that he called her by the nickname.

"When I was maybe six years old, he [her brother] was making us dinner. He was making pancakes for dinner and I didn't want to eat pancakes again so I ran out the back door. He came chasing after me and he was yelling, *you little squirt*!"

During the reading with Kevin, Jennifer couldn't make sense of one scene he was sharing. He mentioned that he could see the La Salette Shrine [the original name for a former religious shrine which was now a gathering place called Turner Hill in the North Shore area of Massachusetts]. That same evening, her husband Jake had met some friends there to play cards. On Jake's way out of his driveway, Kevin told Jennifer that one of the lights

Witness to the World Beyond   185

was out in the driveway and, although he was running late, Jake wrestled with whether or not he should stop to fix that light. He did stop to fix it. Kevin said that was his mother-in-law; she had shut off the light.

Not knowing any of this happened the same evening, Jennifer was perplexed at these remarks. Jake filled her in later that it had happened exactly as Kevin had stated in the reading.

At another point in the reading, Kevin said, "I see blue suits, police and fireman uniforms. Do you have any relatives that are in one of those forces?" She replied that she did not.

Kevin persisted, "Is your husband a policeman? I hear sirens, I see the jaws of life to get him out. He [Jake] was unconscious, the car was totaled."

The accident scenario that Kevin described had occurred to Jake several months prior but he had since recovered and Jennifer oddly didn't recall this during the reading. When Jennifer shared this with her husband, Jake immediately knew – "That's the accident, that's the car accident I was in!"

Jennifer also had brought a picture of her relatives at a family reunion to share with Kevin; it included approximately thirty-five people. He pointed to one of Jennifer's sisters and said, "this one's in trouble, you need to look out for her."

She looked perfectly "vibrant and beautiful" in the picture. She would be the one to later develop severe Parkinson's disease and is currently significantly debilitated.

Jake recalled that Jennifer was still skeptical after she returned home from the reading as she is "skeptical by nature." But after she shared all of the stories with him, and he could piece them together, he was "one hundred percent convinced" as was she. They both hoped to go for a reading again when the pandemic lifted. She laughingly mentioned that their lights "flicker all the time now so we just always assume it's her [Jenn's mother]."

Jake concluded, "You can't make that stuff up. Somebody said to us that he probably researches people. I said you can't research that kind of stuff; you don't know that stuff."

Chapter 14: "You Can't Make This Stuff Up"- More Validation Stories

Wendy Smith is a business owner in her mid-fifties who currently lives with her two grown children as they search for homes to buy for themselves. She first met Kevin in the 1980s when she and a few friends went to his home for medium readings. She didn't recall what he said so long ago but subsequently went to him eight to ten times over the next forty years. They have since become friends and while she occasionally asks him for readings, that is separate from their friendship.

Wendy did vividly recall a reading that involved a conversation that she had with her former husband in the late 1990s. Two weeks prior to that reading, she and her husband had just bought a new home and were lying in bed talking about doing some renovations. It was just "pillow talk" between the two of them. To their left were two windows in the bedroom.

"I would really love to blow those windows out and put like a deck on the outside of this bedroom," Wendy S. said.

"Yeah, some French doors would look really nice," her husband responded.

She had also put some frames on the nightstand. She said at the time, "I can't figure out if I like the silver or gold frame better." She eventually went with the silver.

A few weeks later at the reading with Kevin, he told her, "You have something new going on in your life. Your grandmother is standing behind me and she said that she thinks the French doors would be amazing. And she said the silver frame was a great choice."

"It was just pillow talk between my husband and I. How would he have ever known that? Totally blew me away," Wendy said as she recalled this reading.

Even more amazing to her was a reading that stood out the most over the years, which she referred to as "absolute craziness!" It was about Emma, the unfortunate girl described at the end of Chapter 7, who had jumped off a bridge; Kevin was called in on the case. He saw where they needed to look for her and suggested it would eventually happen on a "five" (he was unsure if this meant day, week or month five at the time), and that a fisherman named Barry would find her while on his boat. As noted earlier, Emma was indeed found on the first day of the fifth week by a fisherman named Barry in the spot that Kevin had identified.

Prior to one of her readings with Kevin, Wendy S. and her husband had separated and were in the process of a divorce. She hadn't yet told Kevin about the breakup. During their courtship, Wendy's husband had shared with her the story of his former girlfriend, Emma. Wendy never knew her; she and her husband began dating well after Emma had passed.

A few days prior to seeing Kevin for this reading at her home, Wendy was clearing out the closet of her soon

Witness to the World Beyond   189

to be ex's belongings. She found a bag of old pictures including a photo album with Emma's pictures in it.

Wendy S. and Kevin were in a private room upstairs while he gave her the reading.

Kevin began with, "Well you have a lot going on in your life. You have some loss…" He alluded to the fact that her marriage was on the rocks.

Then he asked Wendy, "So who is the older woman standing behind you? Her name is Emma."

Wendy S. screamed at the top of her lungs and literally jumped out of her seat. She also recalled she felt goosebumps all over. Her friends, waiting for their own reading downstairs shouted, "What's going on up there?"

"She's not related to you," Kevin stated.

"No, she's not," Wendy agreed.

Wendy S. started to give the backstory to Kevin but he interrupted her, "Wait a minute…"

Kevin realized that it was the same grandmother he had seen when he was first called about her missing granddaughter. The girl's grandmother wanted to make her presence known to Wendy for reasons that were not clear.

Wendy S. shared, "My soon to be ex-husband's phone number was on her cell phone. It was the last number she called."

On another occasion, Kevin stopped by for a quick social visit with Wendy S. at her company's office which is located in an old building in Newburyport, Massachusetts. Wendy had been renting the building for many years from a landlord who had just passed away.

190 Barbara Ellen Mawn

She described her former landlord in the interview, "He was a very distinguished, tall gentleman, about seven feet tall. He always stood with his arms crossed."

When Kevin came in to say hello that day, he greeted her with, "I have to tell you there's a gentleman standing to my left shoulder. He's very tall, has his arms crossed, wrinkled forehead, wears glasses and is very strong looking. He told me, 'Don't worry, I'm just watching over the building.'"

Wendy S. explained who it was without any doubts in her mind. Wendy concluded her interview with the common sentiment, "He's definitely the real deal."

Lauren Torlone, who was first introduced earlier in Chapter 7, shared the story of her sister's reading.

Kevin warned her that, "There's going to be a nurse who has dyed red hair that totally tries to derail your career."

Lauren's sister had been having a problem with her nurse manager but the "red hair" did not fit her description. Until the following week – her manager came in with "fire engine red dyed hair." She ended up having ongoing struggles with this woman but at least it helped her to know that "this person is really bad news." She eventually escaped from her grasp and changed jobs.

Deborah Coull is an esthetician and salon owner in her sixties. She considers herself a friend and promoting agent of Kevin, after knowing him for over thirty years. She clearly remembered the first time she met him. She had gone after work to a friend's house party with Kevin as the medium. She thought he had some kind of tick as he seemed to be pushing away something she could not see.

The first thing he said to Deborah was, "Everybody wants to talk to you!" He then went on to name multiple people she knew who had passed that were in line to speak with her.

She recalled, "It was really amazing; he could name names and describe appearances."

Since that time, she has come to ask him for advice during life crises and at times of major life decisions, including business ventures, surgery options, and buying cars. Prior to the pandemic, she held gatherings at her home for him to read twice a year on average.

"His real talent is giving comfort to people."

Deborah recalled a meaningful reading that has always stayed with her that occurred in the early 1990s while she and Kevin happened to be relaxing at a pool.

"Do you know the name Hunter?" Kevin asked.

"Is it a first name or a last name?" she asked.

"It could be a first, but I think it's a last name."

"No, I don't know anybody, doesn't ring a bell."

"Well, listen for the name Hunter," Kevin advised.

Several months later, Deborah heard of the tragic death of the daughter of a former classmate of hers from town. She felt badly that she didn't know how to get in touch with her former acquaintance anymore to send condolences. Deborah herself was in the process of moving to another city and starting a small business there. She was out doing errands one day and went to several banks to check on loans but enroute home something was telling her to take back roads instead of the more efficient highway route. She stopped at a post office there and ran into the woman whose daughter had died.

192 Barbara Ellen Mawn

Deborah expressed her condolences to her former classmate Paula and apologized that she hadn't gotten in touch with her after she heard the sad news in town because she didn't know where she was living.

"I couldn't find you."

"Well, you wouldn't have been able to find me because I moved and got remarried and my new last name is Hunter," Paula replied.

Deborah said, "I need to speak with you. I have this friend who is a medium."

"I can't believe you're telling me this because today I had an appointment with a medium in Boston. But yesterday she sounded so strange and crazy over the phone that she made me fearful. So, I canceled my appointment with her. I was just saying to my other daughter in the car today that I wished I could find a medium in this area!"

"Well, I think I'm the messenger," Deborah said to her.

Paula's daughter had committed suicide. She had been a dancer and had something wrong with her that caused her great pain that led to her taking her own life. The woman eventually went to Kevin and found great solace. However, he thought it was odd she didn't ever call again until several years later.

Paula called many years later and said to Kevin, "My mother is dying of cancer. Could you please come to the house? I'll pay you whatever you want because I need my mother to hear what you can tell her about those who have passed."

Kevin was flying at the time of the request and couldn't get there for several days. By the time he made it to their home, Paula's mother was still alive but unconscious. The whole family was at her bedside. Kevin

Witness to the World Beyond 193

was able to bring through several people and whether she heard him or not he couldn't be sure but suspected she did. As he was leaving, Paula insisted on paying him higher than his usual charge. He pleaded it was not necessary. She replied:

> "Let me tell you something. You said something to me that didn't make sense to me at the time after my daughter died. You said that I was going to be cleaning out her closet and I was going to find one ballet slipper but I would never find the other one. And that was a sign that she was still there, around me. And I found the one ballet slipper and I never found the other one. You gave me such comfort."

At another medium house party that Deborah hosted, she recalled the story of a friend, Susie, who had recently lost her husband. While Kevin was upstairs giving private readings, her other friends were sitting in her living room, including Susie, with the radio on in the background. The song "It's a Wonderful World" by Louis Armstrong came on.

Susie was astonished and said, "Oh this is a sign from my husband because this was our song. In fact, it was playing on our first date at a restaurant and it was our wedding song."

The group of women all joined in and sang the song with her and then the conversation went back to small group chats among the women. Kevin wasn't present in the room during this occurrence. When it came her turn to go upstairs for a reading, Kevin brought her husband through and gave a few pieces of identifying information about him.

At one point Kevin looked perplexed and said, "Oh my God, you won't believe who's here. Believe it or not, Louis Armstrong is here. Mr. Armstrong will not come in just because you loved his songs. You had to have known him personally."

Susie shared that indeed she did. When she was a little girl, Mr. Armstrong and her parents were best friends. He used to come over every Saturday to their home in New York City.

"He had a nickname for you, Little C. I don't know what that means," Kevin said.

"Yes, he used to call me Little Chief," she responded.

Kevin also recalled a reading with Deborah where she asked his advice on a business venture that she was contemplating but was nervous about securing the necessary bank loan for it.

Kevin said, "All I hear about that are the words *a piece of cake.*"

"What does that mean?" Deborah asked.

"I don't know," Kevin replied.

When Deborah went to the bank with the loan application, the bank officer looked at it and concluded "This will be a piece of cake." She later named her successful new business "Doing Business As (DBA) Piece of Cake."

Liz Baker, introduced in Chapter 11, is a flight attendant who lives in New York, a work colleague, and a close friend of Kevin V. Coan. She is the mother of two grown children and a grandmother of two.

Liz wasn't overly impressed when she heard at work that Kevin was a medium. He didn't showcase it or bring

Witness to the World Beyond   195

it up generally but one day the subject came up as she had heard it through the grapevine. She had been to psychics and mediums in the past but wasn't particularly impressed to hear that he was a medium as "a lot of people say they can do stuff and I was like, yeah, whatever."

Although he has done readings for her throughout the fourteen years they've known each other, she noted, "I don't make that the focus of our friendship. It's like if someone's a baker and you constantly ask, 'Can you make me this? Can you make me that?' You know, it's just not right."

Liz first shared a few back stories during her interview that were related to her realization that Kevin's ability "was real." Months prior to one early reading with Kevin, Liz noticed some decorative pillows in a magazine that had various home decorations on display. As an expert seamstress taught by a master, her grandmother, she declared to herself, "I'm going to make those pillows."

However, she never got to it, even though she had bought the material. Liz also had promised to make ribbons for the bridesmaid's flower in a family wedding. Her daughter-in-law had told her the ribbons should be a foot wide.

Liz disagreed, "No, they're supposed to be only a couple of inches."

Her daughter-in-law was insistent; Liz relented and made the foot-wide ribbons.

One day she stopped for a break in a small tea shop in Boston with Kevin after work.

As they were sipping tea, he casually mentioned, "So, your grandmother's here. She wants to know why you sewed those ribbons wrong when you knew it was wrong. Why did you do it anyway? And why didn't you ever make those pillows? You have the material."

During the interview, Liz recalled thinking, "Oh my God, nobody even knows about that! I mean I had only been thinking about the pillows, that was never verbalized to anyone. And the ribbon thing was between me and my daughter-in-law. I never told anybody! I fell right off my feet. I was like, that's insane, this guy is amazing."

Recently Kevin gave Liz and her sister a phone reading after their father died from COVID-19; she and her sister live in different states.

The first thing Kevin asked Liz on the phone was, "What's with Elvis Presley?"

Liz said, "I don't know."

Her father wasn't a fan of his and no one in the family was a fan. It made no sense to her at the time. Kevin didn't back off.

"Well, your father was with you when you were with Elvis Presley."

Later that night as she went to bed, it hit her. A few days prior, she had some down time on her flight and was editing old pictures, of which she has over four thousand, on her phone.

One old picture in particular struck her and she said to herself at the time, "What a weird place to have a picture of Elvis Presley in a hotel on the island of Aruba."

The photo was taken while she was on vacation in Aruba years ago while waiting for her children to join her the next day.

As she noted in the interview, "The first thing you saw when you walked into this room was a huge picture of Elvis Presley."

So, she had taken a picture at the time and had just laughed about it to herself a few days prior.

She recalled in the interview Kevin's words and her reaction, "Your father was with you when you were with

Elvis Presley. And I'm thinking I never went to see him. But it was when I was looking at the picture of him."

Later during the reading Kevin asked, "Was there a vacuum cleaner in the middle of the kitchen after your father died?"

Liz explained in the interview that before he died, her father had fallen and had to be taken by ambulance to the hospital. When her sister went to his house to clean after his death, there was a vacuum cleaner in the middle of the floor. She thought it odd as he wasn't vacuuming that day but she just put it away. Her sister almost fell off the couch when he mentioned this as she had not told anyone.

Kevin explained, "Your dad was with you [when she found it later after his death] and he had plugged it in the day before and forgotten about it."

Kevin also mentioned to her sister, "You were holding something nautical of your father's. He wasn't in the Navy but had some nautical stuff. Your dad was there when you were packing up his nautical stuff."

Indeed, their father had owned a boat and she had packed up a life vest and a few other boat accessories at his home the day prior to the reading.

Kevin also identified a scene that had just happened to Liz during her most recent phone reading. He noted that Liz lives in an area in New York state that has "tiny blocks, lots of traffic and cars parked on top of each other." Her own driveway is hard to get into as the street itself is very narrow. The day prior to the interview, her neighbor had nearly blocked her in her own driveway.

She was furious and thought to herself, "I'm going to hit this frigging car before I leave!"

Kevin told her in the phone reading, "Your father wants you to know that he was in the car with you last night when you wanted to hit the car and he said - *don't do it!*"

When Liz was born, her father was in the service. The family lived in a trailer in Virginia while he was stationed at Fort Eustis. Liz cherishes a picture from her infancy where her parents are sitting on wooden folding chairs with her outside the trailer near a beach.

Kevin asked about this picture (without ever seeing it) and described it in detail, "Who lived in the trailer park?"

Liz acknowledged that she was born while the family lived in a trailer park.

Kevin replied, "Yeah, they're [her parents] showing me a trailer and wooden chairs and everybody's sitting in the wooden chairs outside the trailer. Yeah, your mother's showing me the picture."

Liz recalled her response, "I'm like, okay."

"Well, they've got nothing else to do," he said, jokingly referring to their relaxed schedules in the afterlife.

Liz also shared the story of her sister, to whom she had given a phone reading from Kevin as a birthday gift one year.

During her sister's reading Kevin said, "Today you were in your living room sitting on your couch and looking at pictures of Joe DiMaggio."

"Oh my God, I was!" Liz's sister dropped the phone.

Earlier that day of the reading, Liz's sister was organizing pictures taken of her family over the past several decades. She had decided to make albums for each of her now adult children. Her husband, the former CEO of a company that supported the Yankees baseball team, often took the kids to watch Joe DiMaggio play and they would get to meet him after the game and have pictures taken. She was having trouble divvying up these pictures,

Witness to the World Beyond 199

so she was holding onto them that day, walking around to the various new albums in progress, saying to herself, "Should I put it here? Should I put it there?"

That comment about Joe DiMaggio was the thing that stuck most in her mind from that reading even though he said "a million other things" that were also on target. For example, he commented that her daughter from Florida would call her soon and he told her what she would have to say. One hour later her daughter called and nearly verbatim told her mother what Kevin had predicted. She was astonished on both counts but in regard to Joe DiMaggio, she was certain that there was "absolutely no way he could know that by himself, no way."

Kevin recalled two stories related to people being in the wrong place at the wrong time. The specificity of his readings led both of the people to have no doubt that Kevin had been in touch with a spirit from beyond. The first story involved a reading at a home with a woman who lived in a seaside town north of Boston. After looking at the picture of a man that one woman showed him, Kevin asked where he had lived and what was his name.

Then he proceeded to tell her, "He was in the Navy. In fact, he was killed while in service to the Navy. He was on the USS Cole and he died during the explosion."

The woman started to appear really agitated and tearful as she exclaimed, "Yes, he was!"

"He was taking his best friend's place and that's why he was killed."

Tears streamed from the woman's eyes at this point.

"As a matter of fact, you married his best friend. But I know that he was really your soul mate."

Kevin was able to "see" and "know" all this information about this stranger from the picture she had brought.

A second "wrong place, wrong time" reading occurred at a public reading event in Beverly, Massachusetts. A woman had brought a picture of her son who had passed.

"I see that your son was killed in Iraq. He (her son's spirit) told me that he took someone else's place that day and was killed."

The woman told Kevin that she didn't know what he was talking about. The army had not told her of any such details. In fact, they had given few details about the circumstances of his death. Several months later, she came to another show of Kevin's – not for a reading herself again but to speak to him afterwards:

> "I just want to tell you that a few weeks after my last reading with you, the doorbell rang. An African American man that I didn't know was at the door. I came to the door. He explained, 'I am alive because of your son. He took my place that day he was killed. I just wanted you to know how grateful I am and how brave your son was.'"

Kevin also recalled a few memorable readings that occurred at his friend Darlyne's office where he often rented a room to do private readings. But initially, he did group readings there with twenty to thirty people in the room. At one group reading, Darlyne herself came in with a broken foot.

Witness to the World Beyond   201

"Your father is looking at your foot and he is laughing," Kevin told her during her reading in front of the group.

"Well, I'm glad he thinks it's funny," She replied with a grin.

"Remember when he broke his foot you were laughing at him?" Kevin asked.

"Ha! You are right. Now Kevin, I have a lot of respect for you but if you can tell me how my father broke his foot, I'll be so impressed."

"Well, I know he was playing softball but a softball didn't break his foot. A golf ball did."

"Oh my God! He was playing softball! He was up to bat and somebody shot off a golf ball from the next field and it landed on his foot and broke it!" Darlyne exclaimed.

At another meeting in Darlyne's office, Kevin recalled a brief story that was painful but evidential. Among the people at the group reading were two young women who were cousins. They came to hear from their grandmother who had passed.

One of the girls asked Kevin, "Can you ask my grandmother about the spring thing? Ask her why do I get sick every spring?"

"Okay, I will ask her," Kevin replied.

Kevin told her that the grandmother responded, "Well I don't know; I was out in the garden."

Kevin told the spirit grandmother, "No, that doesn't answer my question. What's the spring thing?"

Again, the grandmother replied she didn't know, she was out gardening. Kevin brought this information to the girl again and she simply nodded her head silently in front of the group.

After the group reading, the young woman shared with Kevin privately, "Once in a while in the spring I'd stay with my grandmother and grandfather. One spring day my grandfather molested me when my grandmother was out doing the gardening. She always refused to acknowledge it. So technically you were right, she was out doing the gardening."

Elaine Simmons, first introduced in Chapter 12, is married and living with her husband and their daughter. A former restaurant owner, she and her husband sold the business several years ago when he had a health scare. She now bartends part-time in a local Irish pub to keep active and get out of the house. She met Kevin approximately twenty years ago in his medium role through her sister Patty and has since become a close friend. She generally has held a house party where she invites eight to ten people once a year for the past fifteen years. Elaine sets up private individual readings during these house parties. She ensures that everyone has a reading in a separate room, a "quiet place...people always have their privacy."

Elaine had not kept notes from all her readings but recalled a few stories from the past that impacted her. Her last house party with Kevin had just occurred two months prior to the interview; she had taken notes from that event.

The first story Elaine shared though was not from a formal planned reading or house party. Her father had died in November, 2010. She was comforted to see Kevin show up at the wake as a friend. After he stopped at the casket to pay his respects, he came back to her and her sister Patty and asked if he could talk to them for just a moment in private.

He told them, "Your father said, 'Don't worry about the rosary beads. It's okay.' Where he is now, things like that don't matter anymore. He knows you feel really bad Elaine, but don't. He doesn't want you to feel bad because it doesn't matter. Everything's okay."

Elaine had told no one, including her family members, that her mother had once shared that her father wanted to be buried with a certain set of rosary beads when the time came. Elaine knew the ones he wanted but after he died, she had looked everywhere but could not find them. She felt terrible.

As she recalled, "He was very Irish Catholic, a state trooper, very conservative. My father wouldn't ask for a glass of water if his head was on fire! I felt so bad, Dad never asked for anything!"

So, she had to make do and slipped in a pair of rosary beads that she had bought in Ireland, but they were not the ones he had requested. Hearing from Kevin that "it didn't matter" was such a relief.

She shared in the interview, "I felt so guilty and bad because I wanted to fulfill this wish. That was huge to me. That made me feel so much better. That was like crazy because I knew he was talking to my father. There was no other way he would know that."

Elaine's deceased mother and father would frequently "pop in" over the years during Kevin's readings. They each would weigh in on specific events from Elaine's past or present life.

At one reading Kevin said, "Your mother's here and she just screamed, like belted out, 'the wheel!' I don't know what that means."

Elaine of course knew what it meant and she told him. In the interview Elaine explained that she and her mother used to watch the TV show "The Wheel of Fortune" together almost every night. Her mother had nicknamed the show "The Wheel" and that's how the family referred to it.

Kevin then said, "She wants you to know that she knows you still watch the show because you are thinking of her. Every time you watch that show, she's sitting there with you. And she's watching over you, making sure you are okay."

Her mother was also there at the pub one day where she works. Elaine explained that there was a room leading into the office out back where there were cases of beer and some supplies. For several weeks, the room in the back inexplicably smelled like buttered popcorn. Elaine thought it peculiar as she closed up at midnight those weeks, because they did not serve popcorn at the pub.

At one reading Kevin asked Elaine, "What's with the smell of buttered popcorn at the pub?

Elaine said she didn't know.

"Your mother was there. And she knew you smelled it. She wants you to know she was there with you," Kevin told her.

Her mother has also come through to tell Elaine that she knew she had moved into a lovely home after being miserable in her last neighborhood.

"Your mother knows now that you are content. And you're happy. She wants you to know she is happy for you."

Her mother also sent her a message at her most recent reading, "thank you for taking care of everybody."

Elaine was the youngest of five children with only six years between her and the oldest sister. But somehow over the years she has become the one that takes care of everyone. As she noted, "Anytime there's a problem, they come to me."

Witness to the World Beyond   205

Elaine's mother also let Kevin know that, "You're looking at homemade blankets but you won't put them out. She wants you to know that every time you look at those blankets, she's there with you."

Elaine explained that her mother-in-law is an amazing knitter and crocheter. She had made Elaine's husband several blankets when he was sick. She never put them out since as she was afraid something would happen to them. So, she stored them in a closet and once in a while she would simply admire them.

Elaine's father also has come through numerous occasions during Kevin's reading. After she had cut down to two shifts per week after working up to seven days per week for years, her father said, "Tell Elaine that two shifts are enough; don't do any more."

Elaine also suffers from neuropathy in her feet and her father sent the message that he was also sending her healing for her feet. He also was aware that one of his granddaughters had started a sea glass creations business and told Elaine to let her know that he was proud of her. Elaine had never shared that with Kevin.

At her most recent reading, Elaine also heard from her father with an initial cryptic message. Kevin relayed the message, "Shirley Temple. I don't know what that means but your father said 'Shirley Temple.' He wants you to know he was there for that."

Elaine knew exactly what it meant. Recently she had met a single mother at her pub who had just moved to the area. The son was "a very bright young man, I'd say eight-years-old…a very interesting young boy…he and I hit it off and his mom and I have become friends."

Elaine explained that when the boy comes to the pub with his mother, he always wants a Shirley Temple which Elaine initially was not able to make. The bar is more old school, "they don't make cocktails, they serve beer and shots of Jameson."

Over time she has brought in her own cocktail glasses and occasionally offered cocktails with her boss's blessing. She promised the young man she'd make him a Shirley Temple the next time he came in. However, they stopped by sooner than she expected and she didn't have any cherries. At the same time, her husband had stopped by the pub and she asked him to go to the store to buy the cherries, which he did.

After she made it, the boy exclaimed, "This is the best Shirley Temple I have had in my entire life!"

Kevin let her know that her father was there in spirit at the pub with them during this conversation.

While some skeptics will argue that bringing in appreciative and loving deceased relatives is an easy "sell" for some mediums, Kevin does not always bring in positive and loving characteristics from those who have passed.

At one reading with Elaine, Kevin told her, "Harry is here and he's saying he knows he was not a nice man. He knows his son (Elaine's husband) left home at an early age because of that. Harry knows he was a prick and feels bad and he wants everyone to know he is apologizing to everybody. And he knows it was hard on his wife that he was such an asshole."

Elaine had never met Harry, her father-in-law, but "from what my husband tells me, he was not a nice man." Her husband had left home while still in high school to get away from him.

Witness to the World Beyond   207

When Elaine was asked during the interview if this apology brought any comfort to her husband, she recalled he had said, "Well, a little too late for that now, isn't it?"

Kevin also brought in Elaine's grandmother during several readings. One example occurred when she was preparing her house for the most recent medium party with Kevin. Elaine had a conversation with one of her sisters about where to find La-Z-Boy chairs since her sister was looking for one. Elaine told her where a La-Z-Boy store was in the area as she had bought one there for their mother when she was in assisted living. Just a quick conversation, nothing momentous. Kevin had not yet arrived.

When Elaine went into the private room that day for her own reading, Kevin said, "Your grandmother is talking about the La-Z-Boy store. She wants you to know that when you were having that conversation about the store, she was there. And that she is always with you."

Kevin also shared a concern from Elaine's grandmother about Elaine's husband's health. Kevin told her, "Your grandmother asked - Is your husband's blood pressure okay?"

She responded, "I don't know."

She used to check his blood pressure daily after an earlier heart surgery five years ago. But eventually, she recalled that her husband, "being Irish and stoic," asked her to stop.

"I'm fine Elaine, don't worry about me, I'm fine," he tried to assure her.

Elaine laughingly recalled in the interview her grandmother's response through Kevin, "He's kind of stupid. Tell him he has to be careful!"

Elaine spoke of the great impact Kevin has had on her and those who have attended her house parties:

"Every time, he was so right on. Every single person that was there was like 'Wow, I can't even believe this. Are you kidding me?' He brings such relief. I don't know how I would have gotten through my mother's death without talking to Kevin. If I never got those messages, I think I'd still be a basket case. It was life altering to hear that she's okay, that she loves me and is so grateful for what I did for her."

Diane Grimaldi, the nurse therapist mentioned in Chapters 11 and 12, also recalled a story that validated Kevin's uncanny ability to see into her own home through the eyes of her relatives who had passed. On one of her visits to Kevin's office for a reading, she had brought from her hutch a handful of framed pictures of deceased relatives.

Kevin asked, "Were all these pictures taken in front of a waterfall?"

She responded, "no."

"Well, I don't know what this thing is, this waterfall [he turned around and pointed at a window in the office], it's about like this big. And all these people are directly in front of that thing," Kevin replied.

Diane then realized that on a wall behind her hutch, she has a large, decorative, electric, framed moving art piece, the size of a long window that she referred to as a "water feature." It mimics a continuous fountain or waterfall.

Kevin also commented, "Whenever you are there, you are not just in the room with the people you are having dinner with. There is a lot of activity there."

Diane laughed during the interview as she recalled this story as many of her friends have commented at dinner about the dog's odd behavior only in that room. Whenever their dog is there, "He stalks around looking at the walls and at the ceilings, you know how dogs do that when they are looking at something? It's like he's in a trance."

On the topic of dogs, Diane also shared that their last beloved dog was called Bruno. When he died, she and her husband were devastated. They still have a framed picture of him above the couch in the living room, where he was never allowed to sit. A year after Bruno's passing, Diane and her husband were finally ready to get another dog, Dallas. Soon after they purchased Dallas, Diane had a scheduled reading with Kevin and for a lark brought a picture of Bruno.

Immediately Kevin said, "So, this dog has passed on, right? But you have another dog, don't you? This one here [Bruno] wants to know what this other dog [Dallas] is doing on the sofa when he was never allowed to be up there!"

Marie, first introduced in Chapter 11, shared some stories about deceased family members that came through in her readings with Kevin. In one of her earliest readings, Kevin mentioned that he was seeing a man sitting in front of two television sets, but he wasn't sure why or what that meant. Marie knew exactly who that was – an unconventional great uncle. She recalled that her great uncle had two television sets. Each one was broken in its own way – one had no sound and the other had no picture. Not wanting to throw out either one, he watched TV by turning them both on to the same channel at the same time. There isn't any way Kevin or anyone else would have known about that eccentric behavior.

Marie also shared a story about an aunt who came through to Kevin in a reading. Marie found herself responsible for the management of her aunt's healthcare toward the end of her life. This particular aunt was never very nice to Marie growing up but for some reason wanted Marie to take over managing her care at home during her final years. Marie agreed because she was her dad's sister.

At a reading Kevin told her, "Your aunt wants you to know that she did love you and she's sorry for how she acted. She took out her own unhappiness on you and she was so thankful for what you did for her."

Marie recalled that not only were the words comforting but it provided a resolution to her own conflicting feelings about her aunt.

Candice, the critical care married nurse, mother of four children still at home, introduced in Chapters 8 and 11, described a strange message that Kevin once brought through in a reading.

Kevin asked, "Did somebody bring up baby Charlie?" at one of her house parties that both she and a friend attended.

Candice and her friend both cried out, "Oh my God!"

The back story was that she and her friend were working together at a gymnastics clubhouse located in an old warehouse. One warm summer day they had opened the doors to the loading dock area where the parents used to sit and wait for their children's lessons to be over. When Candice and her friend opened the doors to the club, they noticed one of the younger siblings who was waiting with her mother outside. The girl was playing alone near the warehouse docking area and seemed to be talking to herself.

She recalled, "The little girl was playing ball by herself. She's kind of throwing it and she's giggling and laughing all alone."

Candice's friend asked the little girl, 'Who are you playing with, out there?'

"Baby Charlie," she replied.

The little girl then looked at Candice and said, "He's here for you. Baby Charlie knows you."

Candice explained in the interview that her father and grandfather were both named Charles. Her grandmother and aunts always referred to her father as "Baby Charlie." She had explained this coincidence at the time to her friend. When the reference came up again through Kevin at a reading, they were both astonished.

Jennifer and Jake, the married couple mentioned in Chapters 7 and 13, recalled a story that their close friend shared with them after a reading with Kevin at a house party. Their friend had hosted the party and her husband had agreed to a reading. His father had recently passed and he was acutely grieving him. He came out of the private reading room crying. Their friend's husband is a dentist and he had a challenging encounter with one of his young patients that very day. When he entered one of the patient rooms where a young boy and his father were waiting for him, he noticed the window blinds were all dented and broken in several places. They had not been in this condition the last time he had entered that room on that day.

The dentist asked the father of the child, "What happened?"

The father of the child replied, "Nothing."

Kevin brought the dentist's father through in a reading that evening. His father described the incident at his office that day and laughingly said, through Kevin, "The little bastard did it."

At a more recent reading in a private home owned by a woman named Lara, Kevin had the unusual situation of reading five women, four of whom were pregnant and several were related to each other. He said it was a great night, these women were "freaking out" (in a good way) with his reading. But the story that amused him the most was at one point when he brought through Lara's mother.

Kevin explained, "She's standing there. She seemed like a very nice woman. The house was very cute but small. We were in the dining room but the kitchen was close by. All of a sudden, I saw her mother go over and pick up three apples. She started juggling the apples."

"You won't believe what your mother is doing over there. She's juggling apples," he said to Lara.

"Oh my God, my mother used to juggle apples all the time! She didn't juggle anything else but apples!"

Paul M., the high school teacher first introduced in Chapter 7, shared several stories that reflected the theme that "you can't make this stuff up" as well. He recalled his friend Adam who had died of AIDS in the 1990s. They used to meet at the Boston Public Library and then go shopping or out to lunch or dinner. As Adam became sicker, their outings became less frequent.

At one meal Paul recalled that Adam asked him, "When I pass, what do you want? Because it's going to happen to me."

Paul told him that there were two things that he would love to have to remind him of Adam — the wild, large glasses that they bought together in Las Vegas and his long cashmere coat.

One winter, several years later, Paul could not find the coat. He still had the glasses but after looking everywhere in his own home, the closets, the basement and even his mother's house, he could not find the coat.

"Oh, if I lost this coat!" he despaired at the time.

But a reading with Kevin was coming up. Kevin picked up his friend's picture at the house reading and said, "I'm seeing the Boston Public Library. What's this about a coat? He is saying I've got the coat; I've got the coat."

At this point, Paul M. was completely in tune with Kevin's medium abilities and so he asked his friend, through Kevin, "Well where is it?"

At that point Kevin said, "He's standing right behind you."

Paul M. forgot that new people were at this house reading who may or may not believe in Kevin's ability but he didn't care at that point. Paul turned around and yelled at his friend whom he could not see, "WELL, WHERE IS IT? I CAN'T FIND IT!"

He then shared in the interview, "Next day -Boom! It was in the closet."

Kevin shared during his interviews the importance of an evidential mediumship:

"You know there's a lot of sadness out there, a lot of tragedy. People forget the reason why this [mediumship] can be such a good thing, the way it helps people. I can't tell you how many people in my lifetime have told me that I've made a real difference to them."

Part IV: The Impact of Religion and Personal Visits from Spirits

"I have been at work for some time building an apparatus to see if it is possible for personalities which have left this earth to communicate with us."

Thomas Edison (1920)

Chapter 15: Religious Influences on Mediumship Beliefs

Religion did not appear to play a major role in the participants' acceptance of Kevin V. Coan's ability as a medium, despite the conflict with church doctrine that was noted by some of those interviewed. Among the twenty-five individuals who participated in the interviews, thirteen (fifty-two percent) reported that they are currently Christian (nine Catholics, and four non-denominational). In addition, there was one Spiritualist and one Buddhist.

Ten people who reported no current religion included six former Catholics, one who was secular Jewish and one with no religious upbringing. Eight of the participants, (three Catholics, two with no current religion, one Spiritualist, one Buddhist, one non-denominational Christian) discussed actual and potential conflicts that they had observed related to religious dogmas and their belief in a medium. However, that did not cause doubt in their own personal beliefs in legitimate mediums such as Kevin V. Coan. The majority of participants, however, when asked about religious conflicts with mediumship belief were not concerned about or aware of religious prohibitions related to belief in mediums.

Patricia, who is a practicing Catholic, felt that there was no conflict with her religion and her belief in Kevin's ability.

She explained, "It made me firmer in my belief in the afterlife and comforted, just very comforted that he's there [her father], he's watching and seeing what's going on."

Although Alan, who is Jewish but non-practicing, felt that his religion does not recognize spirits beyond life after death, he felt no conflict between his religious upbringing and his belief in Kevin's mediumship abilities.

"It was nothing like that, there was no afterlife, you know? No heaven or hell concept, I wasn't really taught about spirits other than they are in the Old Testament as angels or whatever they were called. I'm pretty sure the Jewish religion teaches you that you are dead and that's it."

While Alan did not experience any conflicts with his religious background, he did add a positive impact on his belief in the spirit world.

"I always had an intense fear of death. And so, this whole thing does sort of help me. How can it even be possible [that spirits exist]? We are here, we are physical – how can it be possible...? I just don't understand it."

But then he recalled that Kevin had advised him, "You don't have to understand it. It just is what it is."

Those who did feel some level of conflict or guilt shared their unique perspectives when asked about religious conflicts.

Sheila Cedrone commented, "It's a contradiction. I mean Catholics do believe in the afterlife. I don't know if they believe in mediums. I don't think so. And I really do believe that what's going to happen is going to happen. You can pray all you want but I think life is random."

Candice L. discussed the "little bit of guilt" that she associates with her belief in mediums as a practicing Catholic. She explained:

> "You're only supposed to believe that this is the way it is and that it's [belief in mediums] out of the realm of what they teach you. Like you can believe in angels, and signs and the stigmata…you can believe all these things but should we really believe that somebody is telling us that they're talking to a loved one that's deceased? I feel like there is a conflict."

Brian Phillips shared his earlier religious upbringing:

> "Well, I was brought up Baptist and anything to do with spirits from the other side was very negative. It was nothing that you ever were to pursue or believe in. So, it was deeply ingrained in me. I just always believed it was hocus-pocus and there was nothing to it. But as I had life experiences, especially with Jeff [his spouse], I would see more instances of believing that there were…that there was another way."

Based on his life experiences, particularly the death of his mother and other close friends, Brian noted, "Through all of these things, I've come to believe that

220 Barbara Ellen Mawn

there is, you know, a spiritual world that we, in daily life, don't know anything about. But I think as people get closer to passing over into the… whatever is next, they are allowed to see, to have a glimpse of what's there."

Marie shared her views on the contradictions within the Catholic Church regarding belief in mediums. When asked if she felt any conflict between her church and her belief in mediums, she replied:

> "I know the church says not to seek out mediums, especially practices of divination but I feel Kevin isn't engaging in fortune telling. Instead, Kevin carefully exercises his abilities as a legitimate, sincere and talented individual who communicates an energy that provides healing and resolution. When I attend a religious service or engage in some type of meditation, I often sense peace or clarity of thought coming through. Kevin's readings provide the same type of experience. I have experienced it myself and have seen it with other individuals being read by Kevin. As such, I personally don't consider Kevin's mediumship in conflict with my own religious beliefs."

Liv Ullmann described herself as a Christian; she was raised as a Lutheran in her home country of Norway. As she described her beliefs related to the metaphysical abilities of mediums, she did not relate it to her religion as such. Rather, she emphasized:

> "What I subscribe to is what I believe in. That there is a higher power and I don't necessarily have to call him God because I think a higher power is so much more incredible than we as human beings can

describe. It's part of everything, everything we do not know. And I don't want to give it a name that has to do with what we understand because we don't understand the higher power. When he's there, and when he lives within us and when he gives power or knowledge to someone like Kevin, it's a higher power."

Although Wendy Golini was raised in the Catholic religion by a mother who was a religious teacher, Wendy turned to the Spiritualist Church in adulthood. She respects other people's religions, many of which she noted do accept the Spiritualist approach which believes in the ability of some people to communicate with those who have passed.

She clarified, "I think the Catholic religion sees it [the afterlife] in an abstract form. Like they talk about it but they don't allow you to acknowledge its true existence."

Wendy G. often gets phone calls from people who are interested in having a reading by Kevin as she is well known for holding these sessions in her home for several decades.

Her experience has taught her that, "When people lose somebody, it's almost like their faith needs confirmation."

She acknowledged that while she still finds comfort in the religion she was raised in, "We existed before Catholicism did, so I know they're [Spirits] here. I know there's something after the existence on earth for sure. I've always been aware of the presence of Spirit around me. So, to me, he [Kevin] is just like kind of a translator."

Although raised a Catholic as a child, Jeff Phillips now follows Buddhist principles as they are more in alignment with his values and beliefs. He went on to explain:

"It's about energy, you can't destroy it; you can't create it. It just changes form. There's a ritual in some sects of Buddhism where when somebody dies, for three days after the person's death, someone is always sitting in the room meditating. The belief is that it takes seventy-two hours for the body to fully release the energy. It's a belief system about energy that you bring to the world and what you do with that energy. This is what Karma is about. Some people leave life with karmic excess – they gave more than they took; they did really good things to help the earth. And then there's others…that leave with karmic debt that has done more damage to people. It's all about learning the lessons of life and refining the energy. I was raised Catholic and you know we believed in the afterlife. But the Church, it's much more categorical, it's heaven or hell. I guess they got rid of limbo [smiles]…but in Buddhism, it's much more dynamic and fluid."

Chapter 16: Messages from Beyond, Not as Uncommon as You Might Think

An unanticipated finding from the interviews was that the majority of the participants shared stories of mystical signs from those that had passed and/or past stories of their own extrasensory perception. While a few believed in the ability to communicate with the dead only because of their readings with Kevin, over half (fourteen) of those interviewed had indeed experienced some forms of communication with the dead on their own.

Alison Blake, first introduced in Chapter 7, was an example of someone who only believed in Kevin's ability through witnessing his work first hand. She acknowledged that she would probably still be a skeptic about mediums if it weren't for knowing Kevin. She needed proof and he had the goods.

"If I didn't see it, you have to see it, you have to. How can you then dispute it? There's just no way you can dispute it."

But others such as Candice, Joe LeBlanc, Brian and Jeff Phillips, Liv Ullmann, Wendy Smith, Nancy, Elaine

Simmons, Patricia, Wendy Golini, Tori, Alan, Paul M. and Deborah Coull had themselves experienced various messages from deceased loved ones.

Candice shared the story of the two entwining hearts that have showed up in her life several times since her grandfather died:

> "My grandfather was a very healthy seventy-three-year-old man who was doing backflips off the diving board before he passed. He passed suddenly on December 21; it was a somber Christmas. Everybody was devasted. My grandfather was such a lovely man. After my grandfather passed, we had the family priest for dinner at my parent's house because in an Italian household, that is what you do. My grandmother kept saying 'I just can't believe it. I can't believe he's gone. I just need to know he's OK.' The family priest said 'Listen, you can always ask for signs and just say a prayer.'
> While my sister and I were getting ready for bed, the priest left, and pretty much all of the family left. There was a little dusting of snow outside. We were both on the other side of the bedroom and all of a sudden one of the pull-down shades just popped up. We both kind of starting laughing and my sister walks over to shut it.
> She said, 'Oh my God!'
> I asked, 'What?'
> At the bottom of my parents' driveway there are two perfectly entwined hearts made in the snow from tire marks but they are not connected. There are no tire marks going in and there are no tire marks going out. We take this picture and call my grandmother and

everybody to tell them. They couldn't see it yet because it was a regular camera and we had to get it developed. The significance was that my grandfather used to sign everything written to my grandmother 'Two hearts, two hearts beat as one.' He'd say that to her all the time.

When my father passed [approximately fourteen months later] in March, maybe two days later, we had a snowstorm. We had all the family over, everybody's crying…and my cousin called and said, 'You need to come outside.' We go down the street, pull out of our mom's driveway and right there are two hearts in the snow. I get those now; I can't tell you how frequently."

Joe Leblanc, mentioned earlier in Chapters 7 and 9, described his experience of sensing those who have passed.

"I know when the spirits are around me, because my ears will start humming, you know what I mean?"

He also acknowledged seeing some of his deceased loved ones on rare occasions.

"After John [his father-in-law] passed, I've seen him once. I've seen Mal [his wife] once, I've never seen my son Joey. At night I see my dog's Spirit and I see a cloud move by me. I asked him [Kevin] what it was. He said it was Marilyn's step-mother, Barb."

Brian Phillips and his husband Jeff shared their own experience of messages from Brian's beloved mother Pat, who had passed away nearly four years prior to the interview.

"From the day Mom passed, I started hearing a bell in our home, not every single day but many, many days in a week. The bell would always be a single tone; it would be in different rooms in the house. It was at different times; it was not a computer, clock or phone; there were no other electronics. When I told Jeff about it, he thought I was a little, you know, maybe I was going through grief or something. He didn't give it much thought until one day he said, 'I'm hearing it now too.' When we decided to sell the house, our realtor was in the house alone showing it one day. She knew about it and she also heard the bell. She later said, 'Brian, your mom was here.' A year to the day when she passed, it stopped; we didn't hear it again. So, it was like for a whole year she wanted us to know I'm here, I know what's going on."

Brian also recalled his mom's visions of "white birds" outside of her hospice room window toward the end of her life.

"My sister and I were there with her and she said, 'Look at those big white birds.' My sister and I turned around and there was not a bird in the sky. Mom was not in a hallucinatory stage or anything like that. She believed that she saw something. In her last few days, she became non-verbal. Jeff was holding her hand one day and she looked up at me and said, 'angels, angels.' Those are the only words she ever said during her last few days."

Prior to being in a non-verbal state toward the end of her life, Brian and his sister took turns visiting "Momma Pat" every day.

Brian recalled:

"My sister came in one day and Mom said, 'Oh you just missed my Aunt Norma.' [their great aunt]. My sister looked at her and said, 'Well you know Aunt Norma isn't with us anymore, right?' Mom said, 'Yeah, I know but she was here visiting for the last hour.' She was convinced that her aunt, whom she was close to, came through and spent time with her. And again, my mom still had her faculties about her, she was not hallucinating."

Jeff Phillip's clairvoyance has been a persistent part of his life. He recalled one of his first visions back in the early 1980s when he lived in California. As he was driving on a tight winding road on the other side of the Golden Gate Bridge from San Francisco in the Marin headlands, he suddenly had this image of a red Miata, a small sports car. Two minutes later as he came around a bend in the road, there was a red Miata that had crashed into the side of the mountain.

Jeff also shared a story that happened more recently, as he was leaving a specialty bakery with a birthday cake in hand:

"I had brought a pair of shoes with me in the car because I was going to return them. I came out of the bakery with the cake and then had another one of those things where I saw a shooting in the men's department [at Macy's]. I saw this guy; he had been shot in the leg and people were flying out the doors screaming. And I thought – there it is again. That night, we're watching the news and in the men's department at Macy's there had been a shooting. One person was shot in the leg. I wondered if that would have been me who got shot; I wonder if these things are protective."

A third example of Jeff's extrasensory perception occurred during his mother's visit with him in California over Christmas, the last Christmas that she would be alive. When she arrived, she was not feeling well but had not yet been diagnosed with the terminal lung cancer that she actually had. Jeff brought her to a doctor friend for an opinion.

The consulting friend said, "I don't have any scans or x-rays, all that I have is the clinical interview and what I listened to during her physical exam. If I didn't know better, I'd have to hazard a guess to say that your mother has lung cancer."

His mother would be formally diagnosed and die from the advanced disease several weeks later after she went home to the east coast. She had visited him on December 23rd and based on the Danish tradition, Jeff went out and bought a tree but didn't decorate until Christmas Eve after she went to bed. Jeff shared this story about that night:

> "I sat bolt upright because I heard my mother screaming. I heard blood curdling screams. I thought she had fallen out of bed so I went flying downstairs and looked in the guest bedroom. My mother was sound asleep. And I thought what was that? It wasn't a dream. I woke up and it was there. So fast forward, my mom gets sick and I spent a lot of time with her in those last weeks. On the morning of her death...she had a metastatic tumor that was pushing into her spinal cord. The oncologist had said, 'If she doesn't get radiation, this will cut her cord. That's a

very painful thing.' The morning of her death, there was the scream. It was exactly the scream that I had heard on Christmas eve, exactly as I remembered it. I sat there and went *Aha!*"

Jeff had been told by a psychic early on during his California days, "You've got the gift but you're afraid of it." When he asked Kevin V. Coan if Kevin sensed any such ability, Kevin also responded, "You do have a very powerful sensitivity."

Liv Ullmann shared that although she had been disappointed that she had not received a message from her former partner right after his death, she did recall an odd occurrence that she had considered at the time to be possibly sent from his "energy." However, it hadn't occurred to her until she discussed this during the interview for this book, that it was indeed a sign that she had missed in relation to her plea to him to show himself in some way after his death. During the interview, she exclaimed that it was the message, - that he had heard her! She recalled that at some point after the funeral, she and her husband flew to Switzerland:

> "My husband was with me and we were in a hotel room in Switzerland. And this is a true story but I never connected it to Ingmar letting me know that he had heard me! Donald said 'Liv, wake up! Look at the table.' And at that table was sitting a bird. And then... the window was open and the bird flew out. And then the bird came in again and just sat at the table. And just sat there. I swear and then it flew out in the end. And I always thought, 'This is the energy of Ingmar.'

Of course, the bird was not Ingmar but the energy….
he took the bird in; he took the bird out. But until
this moment I didn't realize – he was trying to tell me
and he was telling me! But I didn't know what he told
me, but you know why he told me? He told me
because he heard me!"

Years before she had met Kevin, Wendy Smith recalled
seeing and hearing her own mother after she had passed.

"My father died when he was thirty-two. And my
mother raised six kids by herself. My mother passed
away when I was six months pregnant with my first
child. I remember after her services and everything
was settled, maybe one to two days later she came to
me. She said, 'Everything's going to be okay. You're
going to be okay.' I was very pregnant; I almost lost
the baby because of the emotional part of it. It was
incredibly comforting because I couldn't get over it.
I was twenty-two years old; I was young."

Years later, Wendy S. rented space in a very old
building for her business in a seacoast town in
Massachusetts. She used cameras within the building for
security purposes but was surprised to find what they
picked up:

"When I first moved in there, there were so many
orbs that were recorded. It was just fascinating to see
them going in and out of the building, in and out of
the rooms. There were big ones, there were small
ones. I recorded them on my camera because, you
know, they are motion sensored, so I would get an

Witness to the World Beyond   231

alert on my phone. I'd think, 'Why is the motion sensor going off at 2:30 in the morning?' We closed at nine o'clock. I'd go back in the store and pull my cameras up and I'd go, 'What the hell?' Sometimes it was a bug flying by but there were these distinctive orbs going in and out of the building. One time, I was downstairs and I heard the floor crackling like somebody was walking across the floor and my cameras instantly came on. That was the one and only time I got the chills and I said, 'You know what? I'm done. I'm going home. Good night!'" [laughter].

When asked to describe what Wendy meant by orbs, she replied "They were orbs. They're ghosts, but they're white lights."

Nancy had never been aware of signs from the dead before her daughter Amelia passed. But since then, she has experienced what she considered as signs from her.

"One time on our deck I saw a cardinal doing a jig. It was like this bird was hopping up and down and all around [mimics dancing moves while laughing], these really kind of silly maneuvers. And I can remember being so shocked and I don't know, it was like I felt a chill. I have that feeling sometime like I'm going to see something and I don't know if I stop myself from seeing it because I don't know if the people that we love would want to scare us!" [laughs].

Nancy also shared her husband's vision, "I haven't seen her yet although my husband said to me one morning, 'This is crazy. I don't think I dreamt it but I saw a display of fireworks in our hallway and Amelia was there.'"

Nancy acknowledged that their friends who have experienced great loss have also shared that they have felt somebody rubbing their backs when they felt particularly despondent. Or radio channels would inexplicably change when in the car to a favorite song of their loved one that had passed.

"I've seen things like that. A lot of times flickering lights, you know, you'll be driving along the road in [their town] and every single light will go off as you go by it. But I had to be ready to see those signs, be in a good place. Because at first, I think you're either frozen or scared."

Elaine Simmons shared her personal experiences with the spirit world:

> "I feel like I can feel spirits. And I always say I don't want to see you because that would like freak me out. But it's not scary. I just have this sense; it's hard to describe. And sometimes if I'm like trying to sleep I tell them to go away, I don't want you here right now. I can't deal. It doesn't happen very often for me."

Patricia recalled a message that she felt strongly was from her deceased father on a day that she sorely needed it. He had died one month after having a major stroke. They had made many decisions about not to extend his life at the end as they thought that was his wish but they never had held that discussion with him. As the family nurse, Patricia was the driver of the decision to put him on hospice toward the end rather than choosing aggressive treatment to prolong his life and suffering.

Witness to the World Beyond   233

She was driving to her mother's house several weeks later to meet her brother so that they could help update their mother's health care proxy form, now that her husband had passed.

"You know it's funny, after my father died, and I was very close to my father…I was driving down to my mother's house and I'm talking to him, 'Dad, you know I can't believe you're not giving me any signs. Did I do enough? Should I somehow have done more to support you? Was there anything else we could have done?' So, I get to the house after having these thoughts the whole way down. I go into his file cabinet where he had copies of their health care proxy forms. In this file, I find a folded up legal document that he had gone to a lawyer for. He had them write something up that said, 'I want no feeding tubes, no life support that will keep me alive.' I said to my brother, as I burst out crying, 'I was just feeling so terrible and Dad wasn't giving me any signs. I was feeling like maybe we made mistakes. Did we do everything the right way? And look what I find!' He said, 'The whole way here I was thinking the same thing.' So, it was just like my father knew we needed that."

Patricia also shared one psychic dream that she had which involved a close friend who had a "crazy haircut" in a dream. When she shared the dream with him the next day, he said, "No, I didn't get any crazy haircuts."

That very day he was in a car accident where one of his friends was killed. He survived but "ended up waking up to the nurses shaving his head so that they could suture him."

Wendy Golini, as noted in the prior chapter, has always been aware of the presence of spirits. Many of the people in her family have been known to have "intuitive" abilities, including at least one of her sisters, her sons and herself. She describes herself as open to spirit communication but that what she has is something that everybody slightly possesses.

She noted that communication with spirits requires practice and not everyone has the same level of ability.

"I'll never be Kevin but it's ideal that as long as I'm around people like Kevin, I'm very good at receiving them as an interpreter."

Wendy G. shared a sign from her mother that both she and her brother have consistently received since her passing. Their mother was a puppeteer and had written a play about a rabbit that wanted wings. She had told Wendy that when she died, she wanted to be buried with the rabbit puppet from that play. Despite the consternation of her father, who thought it was ridiculous, her mother was buried along with her rabbit puppet. The day after her mother passed, a brown rabbit appeared on Wendy G's front lawn.

When her brother got home that day, he called her and said, "You're not going to believe this but there's a white rabbit waiting for me in my yard."

During one reading Kevin mentioned to Wendy, "You've been looking at rabbit puppets while thinking of your mother."

"Yes," she acknowledged and reminded Kevin that her mother was buried with her beloved rabbit puppet.

"No, I'm not talking about that one. You will go to a store soon and try to buy a rabbit puppet but the price tag will be torn," Kevin said.

A few weeks later Wendy was shopping at a Barnes and Noble bookstore in the children's section and saw a rabbit puppet. Of course, she was drawn to buy it.

At the register however the clerk said, "Well I can't see the price, the tag is torn. I have to call my supervisor."

Wendy remembered with a smile Kevin's reading and purchased the rabbit puppet once the price was determined.

While several people shared that they or their family member may have actually seen a spirit, or received such signs as the rabbit, Wendy G. described two instances that she could only explain as an actual visit from spirits who appeared to be visible. It was only after their interaction with her that she came to the conclusion that they were spirit apparitions sent to share a message with her.

The first example occurred during the trying experience of going for legal custody of her son whom she later adopted, described in Chapter 12. The day before Wendy's emergency court hearing about custody, she left her lawyer's office inconsolable with grief and worry about the hearing. She first went to the cemetery where her brother David was buried.

She prayed to her brother's grave aloud.

"I can't take this because I'm going to lose my restaurant… but I will not stop fighting for my child. I am just so tired. I wish we were kids again down the park. I can't take this. I don't have it in my heart."

Soon thereafter she left the cemetery and had to drag herself back to work that night at the restaurant. When she arrived, she realized she also had a neighborhood friend's wake to attend before she started her evening management shift at the restaurant. She shared this story about the evening before the court hearing:

"You know when you are very distraught, I'm a very strong-minded woman but I was now in a very vulnerable moment. A couple walked in. The woman was very large. She had a robe on, white hair, wearing gorgeous crystals. I love crystals. And she's with a gentleman whom I could best describe as looking like Sam Elliot with the gray hair, the mustache, the bolero…the whole nine yards. I looked at them and said, 'You're not from Melrose.' They looked at each other and smiled and said, 'No, we are not.' I looked at the woman's neck and said, 'That's a beautiful crystal.' She grabbed my hand and wrapped it around the crystal and said, 'do not worry, tomorrow all your problems will be solved.'"

Wendy G. was next aware that one of her servers was calling her over to see several of her neighborhood friends (whom she and her brother used to hang out with at the park) that had come from the wake to see her. Wendy bid good bye to the mysterious couple.

Seeing all her friends there to comfort her about her upcoming legal battle, her server said, "We're here, we've got this."

Wendy was then able to take a needed respite with her friends on the patio. Her servers were like family to her; they were aware of her challenging court case the next day.

She recalled:

"Before I knew it, every single person I knew that I had grown up with in the park was surrounding me. They all came in. So now, later, when I go to close the restaurant, I asked, 'How did the people at table four enjoy everything?' My server said to me, 'What are you talking about?' So now I think I'm losing my mind. I said, 'the couple I was talking to over there.' And they said, 'No, Momma, no one like that was there, no one came in like that.' Ok, I guess I'm delirious!" [she laughs].

The next day in court, as the judge entered the courtroom, Wendy G. did a double take. The judge was a large woman wearing a black robe and except for the color of the robes, "...without a doubt, because of the absolute size and demeanor when the judge came out, you could have substituted one for the other." [referring to the woman wearing crystals at the restaurant].

The restaurant table where the mysterious visitors were seated during the evening before was the same spot where the court-assigned lawyer for the child had eaten when she had visited the restaurant, months prior. Wendy had no doubt in hindsight that the apparitions that only she saw and spoke to at that table were Spirits sent to her by her brother to give her peace and strength for the upcoming court battle. And she firmly believed that he had somehow managed to send in their childhood friends from the park to her in her time of need as well.

The second apparition that Wendy G. reported to see in the flesh occurred in the kitchen of their restaurant several years after the emergency court date. She and her husband had been arguing about his insistence on selling their restaurant for the sake of their marriage. She was not in favor of doing it after all the hard work they had both put into making it such a success. But she reluctantly agreed to sell it in order to salvage the marriage.

As she noted, "Selling a restaurant is as difficult as opening a restaurant."

On this particular day she was upset about the decision to sell and the hassle of trying to sell it. Wendy was coming back from the market and once again, she stopped at her brother David's grave because she was so frustrated. Once she arrived back at the restaurant:

> "My husband and I were in the kitchen; the back door was open. We are arguing and all of a sudden, a guy pops in with white hair, crazy white hair again. I said, 'Excuse me, can I help you?' He said, 'You want to buy some olive oil?' I said, 'What?' He's like, 'Olive oil.' My husband just yells something at me and goes downstairs into the office. I said, 'Sir, this isn't really a good time. Do you mind?' I didn't want to be rude to him. So, he replied, 'Well can I give you my card?' 'Absolutely,' I said. So, on the front of this card, it's a business card, it says: Rocky, knowledge and wisdom my best resource. We serve those in need in many ways. Have faith and trust. Save so you can make money. Where it comes to your mind, service is the heart of our business. To solve your problems, your problem is our problem to get better. Results in the end, in the long run. On the back, he hand-wrote Olive Oil with his phone number. He also wrote,
> 'We buy and sell consignment, we reach out with information, we are helpful to send you to the right people. We will try to do our best to get a buyer for you and a categorical solution. It costs you nothing to speak to Rocky. Just call me.'"

Witness to the World Beyond   239

This was the second time in her life that Wendy did not immediately realize that what she saw was a spirit, sent soon after a visit to her brother's grave. She thought it odd initially – the man had no olive oil samples, nothing to show, no printed information about his product or name of his company, - just the unusual card. She still has the card which she has kept since 2004. She recalls not calling the number for a long time as it had dawned on her soon after the encounter that trying to call him was not the point of the visit. When she finally tried the number, it did not exist. She wasn't surprised.

Not too long afterwards Kevin came to visit her, as by now they were good friends. They were sitting on her back patio when Kevin noticed that she was not relaxed. She explained that they finally had gotten a buyer with validated finances for the restaurant but she was still stressed about the pending mountain of paperwork.

She happily exclaimed, "We are finally going to do it!"

And Kevin responded, "Hmmm, yeah….no, that guy is not going to get the financing."

She said, "Kevin, shut up!"

She laughed recalling this as she responded, "No!!!"

Kevin insisted, "I'm telling you, the guy's going to have problems with the financing."

"Oh Kevin, I can't…like my business is going to go down south because people are going to think we are gone."

He said again, "But don't worry. The Mexicans are coming."

"Kevin, stop it. I have an Italian restaurant and someone's going to buy it who's Mexican?"

Kevin responded, "Allright, allright, whatever… just remember I said that."

As it turned out, Kevin was correct; the sale fell through. Soon thereafter another potential buyer came along and put up earnest money to buy the restaurant. It was not someone of Mexican descent. Wendy was relieved that this buyer seemed like a sure thing.

One day as Wendy was shopping in Target, her realtor called her and asked, "Are you sitting down?"

"No, I'm in a store!" she replied.

He explained the situation despite her standing posture. The second buyer had changed his mind. He wanted out of the deal even though it had been in progress for thirty days. Wendy G's knee started to finally drop as she slumped to the floor at Target.

The realtor then asked, "Well can you get back to the restaurant right now?"

"Why?"

He responded, "Because I have two people in my office, two unsolicited people came in today looking to buy a space to expand. Yeah, two Mexican guys are in your restaurant right now having lunch. Can you get there?"

Wendy G. rushed to the restaurant and had the signed paperwork within twenty-four hours. They later turned her Italian restaurant into a Mexican restaurant.

She laughingly told Kevin after that deal finally went through, "All right, I'm not doubting you anymore."

Wendy then shared in the interview, "I have to tell you, I lost all fear of the future at that point. I became fearless after that, fearless because I know they're [Spirits] there, they are helping in a serendipitous way."

Tori noted that Spirits may come to us in the form of dreams. She shared that she had experienced "a lot of really profound dreams which feel more like visits from people who have died. It's interesting, like this whole other kind of world and being open to those type of messages. It's kind of like you've got to find the right radio frequency."

Paul M. shared a vision he had which, at first, he could not explain. Two summers prior to the interview, during the height of the COVID-19 pandemic, he was walking down his hall toward the kitchen when a flash of bright light hit him in the eyes. He assumed it was a reflection of light from a car that hit the window. It was daylight; he never mentioned it to anyone. A few days later, he attended a reading by Kevin in a friend's back yard where all safety precautions were used, including masks and safe distances between people. When it was his turn to be read Kevin asked, "Did you see a flash of light recently? I mean just like a few days ago." Paul responded yes, that he had.

"That was your brother," Kevin told him.

Paul recalls telling Kevin:

"I'm going to stop you right there and say thank you. If you look up to the sun and you look away, you see a sun dot. If someone flashes a square light, like a neon light, you see that neon light after. I saw a flash; it was all glowing like a head and a shoulder. That's what I saw when that flashed. When something flashes you close your eyes and you can still see it. That image was stuck. I didn't think anything of it, but now I do."

Paul M. also shared an unexplainable occurrence that he later attributed to his deceased mother's intervention. After having surgery one year, he was prescribed short term pain medications. He had a trip planned and was certain that he had packed the pain killers in one of his two bags. He had a carry-on suitcase in the plane overhead compartment and carried a small blue backpack bag in front of him.

When his pain returned at the beginning of the flight, he went to get his small medicine bag out of his backpack. It wasn't there; he assumed that he must have stuck it in the larger carry-on. He waited until he arrived at the airport to search the carry-on suitcase. The medicine bag was not to be found. He checked his smaller carry-on backpack again – the medicine bag was not to be found anywhere. He searched both bags inside and out.

When he arrived at his destination, he called his roommate and asked him to check everywhere for the little blue medicine bag at home so that he could overnight it to him. But it was nowhere in their apartment. In his own mind as he was talking to his roommate, Paul M. recalled saying to his deceased mother in frustration, "Ma, I just wish you could pick the medicine up and put it at the front door and ring the bell. I'll open the door and that's where it will be."

Just after this thought he told his roommate he was going to check his bags one more time.

"I go through the backpack bag and boom da da boom! There's one small book in the bag, I move it and the blue medicine bag is behind it now. There's no way I missed this. I know me. There was no way I missed this earlier!"

Two weeks later Paul M. had a reading with Kevin and told him about this occurrence.

"Can that stuff really happen?" he asked Kevin, meaning did his mother really place his medication in his bag after the fact?

Kevin responded, "Oh absolutely, that's what happened."

Paul M. replied, "Kevin since you're telling me that, and I have known you now for almost thirty years and you haven't said yes to everything I've asked…I'm going to say, 'Thanks Ma.' And so… what are the lottery numbers? Just write them down!" [laughing as he recalls this in the interview].

But he said that in jest; he knows that is not how it works and that it is not even remotely related to the purpose of Kevin's ability.

Alan shared that he had experienced a "haunting" in his apartment in 2008. He had been having weird things happen in his bedroom, which later matched the experiences of a friend who had previously occupied this same room.

> "I was lying in bed and I always listen to my radio as I go to sleep. And suddenly I realized it was turned off. I didn't have a timer on. It had already happened before – these weird experiences with the radio. The room was dark and I was like 'Okay, if you turned that off, turn it back on.' And it came right back on! I freaked out, freaked out. My cat was on the bed and he suddenly looked up at something and watched it like it was going out of the room."

A few days later Alan was scheduled for a reading with Kevin. Kevin said to him, "When you were in your bedroom, did something happen to your radio the other night? Well, your grandmother, I can't say it was your grandmother that did it, but she knows about it. Is yours the bedroom with the lighter walls in the apartment?"

Alan replied, "yes."

"Well, it's not a bad ghost," Kevin assured him.

Deborah Coull shared her childhood reputation as being "highly visual, I'm a visionary." She acknowledged that she saw people in spirit form as a child.

> "My elderly great aunt would say when I was a kid 'Have you heard anything today? Did you meet anybody today?' I didn't know what was going on, but you know, I knew…I remember once when we had a family tragedy and I stayed with another family. It was a hot, hot July night and Johnny Carson was on. I was in the living room, sitting in one chair and they were doing anything to give me some comfort. Generally, when Spirit would sort of poke me, there would be a noise or clap or something. I heard this clap and looked over at the husband of the couple. He was sitting on a chair but I could see this gray matter head and shoulders plant his hands in the chair and lift himself up at 11:30 pm. So, I said [to the husband sitting in the chair], 'Neil you're sitting on…someone.' The next day at breakfast he asked, 'Did you tell Fay what you saw?' I told her and she said, 'That was my father's chair and every night at 11:30 after Johnny Carson, he would put his hands on the chair and lift himself up because his legs were bad and go to bed.' And I said, well, he was sitting on it last night, he was there!" [laughed when recalling this story].

Toward the end of the interview with Deborah, the next steps of publishing were mentioned and the interviewer jokingly mentioned that she hoped Kevin's Spirits would help in that regard. Then she mentioned she felt chills as she said that and Deborah said she too just got the chills.

"Yeah, it went right through me too [goosebumps and chills] and that's my sign."

Afterword

"At some future day it will be proved, I cannot say when and where, that the human soul is, while in earth life, already in an uninterrupted communication with those living in another world."

Immanuel Kant (1766)

While some may argue that a belief in communication with spirits from the afterlife may be wishful thinking among the poorly educated, even the great philosopher Emmanuel Kant struggled to explain the nature of spirits and the afterlife. He was well aware of the claims of Emanuel Swedenborg, the contemporary scientist and seer who was briefly mentioned in Chapter 3 as one of the first great mediums. Kant dissected Swedenborg's ability to communicate with past spirits in his 1776 book "Dreams of a Spirit Seer." A rational man, Kant could not come to a conclusion about the limited knowledge that we have of the metaphysical world. As his famous quote on the first page of this section suggests, some day we will better understand the nature of communication with a spirit world.

I had no doubts of the veracity of the stories shared by Kevin V. Coan and those interviewed for this book. I had already learned from four readings with Kevin myself over the past decade that he can identify evidence that only exists in my memory. And I know for certain that he would never attempt a google search in any case.

In addition to Kevin V. Coan, the participants that I personally interviewed for this book consisted of seventeen women and eight men with an average age of sixty and a range of twenty-nine to eighty-three years. Their homes were located in two countries, the United States (US) and Norway. Those from the US lived in five different states within the northeast region.

The educational level of those interviewed ranged from high school diplomas to some college, to bachelor degrees, to PhDs and post-doctoral fellowships. One was the recipient of eighteen honorary doctorates. They came from all walks of life. They consisted of current or former bricklayers, nurses, aestheticians, advanced practice nurse psychotherapists, business owners, radio/tv personalities, flight attendants, teachers, mortgage bankers, inventory control specialists, information technology (IT) specialists, data engineers, newspaper marketing specialists, actors, directors, authors, paralegals, legal compliance experts, bartenders, chocolatiers and restauranteurs. The majority were still working, thirteen full-time and six part-time; six were retired.

The range in the number of readings given to these individuals by Kevin V. Coan was from one to seventy-five readings, with an average of eleven readings. Some of the participants had only known Kevin for a few months and several had become friends over several decades after knowing him as a medium initially. They each shared their personal losses and stories about Kevin V. Coan's impact on their lives along with some laughter and tears shed during our phone and zoom interviews.

The recurrent themes from the stories shared by the twenty five participants in this project included validation, clarity, peace, forgiveness, conflict resolution, reassurance, understanding, and catharsis as a result of Kevin's ability that he shared with each of them. I then organized these themes into the broader chapter categories in Part III.

Repeatedly I heard in the validation stories, "There is no way he could have known that…" Kevin V. Coan has given solace to thousands of people that he has read over his lifetime, an astounding contribution and legacy for such an unassuming man.

I had learned that stories are indeed a unique form of data during my academic training. For this project, I followed a clear and systematic method of collecting data learned during my qualitative research method training. I used open-ended questions that I tried to keep as neutral as possible in order to eliminate or introduce any bias. I used a loosely structured interview guide to facilitate dialog and allow "unasked information" to enter the conversation. I audiotaped all interviews and transcribed them verbatim to ensure that I had the words of the participant in front of me when I either used a direct quote or paraphrased parts of their stories.

A few odd things happened along the way in the process of gathering the information for this book. Many

250 Barbara Ellen Mawn

of the participants choked up or became tearful as they recalled the events of their past during the interviews. Some asked to stop for a few moments and others just sobbed quietly through some of their recalled losses. However, there were many lighter moments and shared laughter during the interviews as well. Wendy G's sighting of a FedEx truck in her neighborhood during our interview comes to my mind with a smile. She was in the process of telling me the story of her deceased brother who had told her through Kevin V. Coan, that he commandeered several FedEx trucks during one of her most trying days at court to obtain custody of the child that she had raised. And there in her view out the window of her home was a FedEx truck as we spoke. And yes, you might think that FedEx trucks were ubiquitous during the height of the pandemic when I conducted most of the interviews, but still, she was certain that it was another greeting from her beloved brother. And I did not doubt her as we laughed heartily at the coincidence or possible message from beyond.

I also noted in the last chapter that I "felt chills" when talking about my wishful thinking about Kevin's spirit guides helping to get this book published. At other times, however, specifically during the interviews with Nancy, Brian and Jeff, I felt the sensation of the loved one who had passed very strongly at times during the interview. It came as a sudden sensation of chills and goosebumps all over. I did share that feeling of connectedness with the participant's loved one at the time. It simply felt like the right thing to do; those interviewed were neither alarmed not doubtful and indeed, all were happy to hear it.

The night before the interview with Jennifer and Jake, another odd thing happened. I had a vivid dream about a much beloved cousin, Gerry Beauchamp, who had died that same week, four years prior. I hadn't thought of him in quite some time and had never dreamed about him. During Jennifer and Jake's interview the next morning, they mentioned the Massachusetts town in the North Shore where they lived, which was where my cousin was from. I broke from my script and simply asked them if they had known him perchance. They knew him and in fact Jennifer was close friends with his wife. Coincidence perhaps, but a strange coincidence.

And so, these feelings of connection that I experienced at times during this project had not been anticipated. My low level of paranormal ability is no doubt not as strong as my Irish grandmother's and not even close to the realm of Kevin V. Coan's abilities. But as noted in the final chapter, communication from beyond is apparently not uncommon. It is my hope that the readers of this book will be open to these messages of love and comfort in their own lives.

Acknowledgements

I would like to acknowledge my grandmother, Nellie Mawn, for being the first to suggest that there could be a spirit or metaphysical world right in front of our eyes. Also, I am indebted to my own parents, Ann and Everett Mawn, who have always supported my chosen, sometimes non-traditional paths in life and for communicating with me from beyond on occasion. I only hope that I can inspire a world of spiritual contemplation in my own granddaughters, Annie and Teagan. My children, Brendan and wife Kelly, Chris and partner Liz, and Carolyn and fiancé Paul, have provided love and support throughout this rather unusual turn from pediatric emergency room nurse, to academic researcher and professor, to biographer/storyteller.

My extended family of six siblings, their partners and too-many-to-count much beloved nieces and nephews have also provided me with encouragement and support throughout the writing of this book. I thank my sister Bonnie for her enthusiasm about this project and her willingness to be a first reader. My second editor, George, also contributed quite substantially to this book. My oldest friend (since age five!) Marylou Fierro was an expert editor during the final phase of the project. And many thanks to my former Thai student and now colleague, Dr. Nipaporn Butsing, who helped me with the formatting. I am indebted to each of my editors and supporters for their generous offer to assist me. Any errors that remain are my own responsibility. My childhood friend Brenda Pizzo, an author in her own right, provided ongoing support and advice on publishing. I was also fortunate to have a core support group of fellow writers from the Brandeis Writer's Guild who read draft sections and have been very encouraging with this project.

But of course, the book would not be possible without the collaboration of Kevin V. Coan, despite his busy schedule and initial reluctance about the project. Not one to want the spotlight shined upon him, he was willing to share many painful and proud moments of his life during several formal interviews and many subsequent informal chats. I feel honored to consider him now as a good friend in addition to collaborator.

Each of the twenty-five interviewed participants who shared their stories provided the evidence of Kevin's ability as a medium and revealed the impact that he has made on their lives. Without the generous giving of their time and sharing of life stories, there would be no evidence to present, no book to be written. They willingly recalled many sorrowful and uplifting memories in order to validate the work of Kevin V. Coan. They were truly committed to helping this book take form out of respect for Kevin's work, particularly in light of his humble and unassuming demeanor. As previously noted, Kevin does not refer to his ability as a gift but those who shared their stories let me know in no uncertain terms that he was a gift and a blessing to them during their time of great sorrow and healing.

Printed in Great Britain
by Amazon